THE HOME BARTENDER

Over 125 Drinks with Four Ingredients or Less

SHANE CARLEY

Author of *The Mason Jar Cocktail Companion*

CIDER MILL
PRESS

BOOK
PUBLISHERS
Kennebunkport, Maine

THE HOME BARTENDER

13-Digit ISBN: 978-1604336122
10-Digit ISBN: 1604336129

This book may be ordered by mail from the publisher. Please include $4.95 for postage and handling. Please support your local bookseller first!

Books published by Cider Mill Press Book Publishers are available at special discounts for bulk purchases in the United States by corporations, institutions, and other organizations. For more information, please contact the publisher.

Cider Mill Press Book Publishers
"Where good books are ready for press"
12 Spring Street, PO Box 454
Kennebunkport, Maine 04046

Visit us on the Web! www.cidermillpress.com

Cover design by Shelby Newsted; interior design by Jaime Christopher

Photos by Appleseed Press Book Publishers: Cover, and pages 1, 2, 3, 18, 19, 74, 75, 102, 106, 108, 116, 118, 119, 132, 138, 139, 148, 154, 155, 156, 158, 174, 175, 190, 192, 202, 206, 207, 240, 246, 250, 256, 258, 259, 260, 266, 268, 270, and 272.

Photos by Shutterstock: pages 6 (Daria Minaeva), 10 (Nikolay Litov), 13 (Joshua Resnick), 15 (Ivan Mateev), 16 (Palmer Kane LLC), 21 (gresei), 23 (alexpro9500), 24 (Rob Stark), 27 (Yeko Photo Studio), 28 and 31 (Brent Hofacker), 32 (melis), 35 (Ivan Mateev), 36 (bogdanhoda), 39 (Shulevskyy Volodymyr), 40 (Arina P Habich), 43 (Andrew Pustiakin), 44 and 47 (Sea Wave), 49 (Mark Skalny), 50 (Ramon L. Farinos), 53 (Olena Kaminetska), 55 (Julie208), 56 (graphia), 59 (Cristi Lucaci), 60 (Tomophafan), 62 and 65 (Brent Hofacker), 66 (bitt24), 68 (Evgeny Starkov), 71 (gresei), 72 (Scaffer), 76 (Natalia Bratslavsky), 79 and 80 (Ivan Mateev), 83 (verca), 84 (Pinkcandy), 87 (kaband), 88 (Mateusz Gzik), 90 (Gregory Gerber), 92 (Brent Hofacker), 94 (Iryna Pospikh), 96 (Oksana Shufrych), 98 (Olga Miltsova), 101 (baibaz), 105 (Igor Normann), 109 (Wollertz), 110 and 111 (gresei), 115 (osov), 120 (Champiofoto), 122 (Palmer Kane LLC), 124 (3523studio), 127 (Ivan Mateev), 128 (Wollertz), 131 (martiapunts), 135 (Wollertz), 136 (3523studio), 140 and 143 (Wollertz), 145 (yasuhiro amano), 146 (Palmer Kane LLC), 147 (Wollertz), 150 (apolonia), 161 (Wollertz), 162 (Christopher Elwell), 165 (Poznyakov), 157 (Tom Bartlett), 158 (Leon Rafael), 170 (Danny E Hooks), 176 (vrjoyner), 179 (alexpro9500), 181 (stockcreations), 183 (Martin Vecera), 184 (vsl), 187 (Vahan Abrahamyan), 188 (sanneberg), 193 (Tanya Brighidina), 195 (merc67), 196 (Paul Binet), 199 (Mateusz Gzik), 200 (Angel Simon), 205 (galS), 208 (Al Nemer Olena), 210 and 214 (viennetta), 213 (sanneberg), 216 (Wollertz), 219 (HandmadePictures), 220 (Jeff Wasserman), 222 (sanneberg), 224 (Wollertz), 226 (3523studio), 229 (Mateusz Gzik), 230 (Wollertz), 232 and 234 (Brent Hofacker), 236 (Africa Studio), 239 (RubinowaDama), 243 (Stolyevych Yuliya), 244 (Joshua Resnick), 248 (Prazis), 254 (French), 262 (Scruggelgreen), 263 (Glenn Price), and 264 (graphia).

Glassware icons by Shutterstock; all ingredient icons by Shutterstock or Appleseed Press Book Publishers.

Printed in China

2 3 4 5 6 7 8 9 0

CONTENTS

3

INTRODUCTION

Cocktails can be complicated. With so many drinks featuring what feels like dozens of ingredients, being mixed together in increasingly complicated and diverse ways, it isn't hard to feel out of your depth when it comes to mixology.

But it doesn't have to be that way! Some of the best cocktails in the world feature only a couple of ingredients, shaken or stirred together in simple proportions and ready to drink in seconds. Everyone knows that sometimes simplicity is the way to go—not just for the sake of convenience but for taste as well. After all, who needs eight different ingredients muddling their flavors together when all you really want is something to accent the great taste of your whiskey or rum?

You'll see the terms Classic, Perfect, and Budget being thrown around this book. Their meanings are simple: the Classic version of a drink is a by-the-book version that you can't go wrong with. The Perfect version is a drink made with only the best ingredients. And the Budget version is a more simple, affordable cocktail that will still taste great.

The Home Bartender features the best of the best when it comes to simple cocktails. With classic cocktails you'll recognize and new drinks you're sure to love, there's something for everyone here. Whether you're looking for some new vodka drinks or looking to bust out an old tequila recipe, *The Home Bartender* is the perfect book for any home bar!

BUILDING YOUR HOME BAR

When it comes to mixology, you should never feel like you have to spend hundreds of dollars on obscure liqueurs just to mix a cocktail you might drink once a month. As long as you have the basics covered, you should feel pretty good! The truth is, while some exotic cocktails might call for specialty ingredients like Chambord or crème de cassis, you'd be surprised how many perfectly delicious drinks can be made with good old-fashioned whiskey, gin, vodka, tequila, and rum.

That said, there are ingredients that are more common than others, and adding a few flavorful liqueurs to your home bar will give you options you might never have considered. From coconut rum to orange liqueur, these are the basics that can help you build a home bar that will impress your guests, with options ranging from bargain bin must-haves to top-shelf favorites.

BASIC BOTTLES

Vodka
Budget: Svedka

Classic: Skyy

Perfect: Grey Goose

Gin
Budget: Seagrams

Classic: Tanqueray

Perfect: Bombay Sapphire

Rum
Budget: Bacardi

Classic: Captain Morgan

Perfect: El Dorado

Tequila
Budget: Agavales

Classic: Jose Cuervo

Perfect: 1800

Whiskey
Budget: Evan Williams

Classic: Maker's Mark

Perfect: Woodford Reserve

Must-Have Mixers
Triple Sec

Sweet Vermouth

Lime Juice

Lemon Juice

Bitters

Grenadine

Simple Syrup

Nice to Have
Dry Vermouth

Kahlua

Crème de Menthe

Malibu Coconut Rum

Blue Curacao

Wish List
Campari

Orgeat Syrup

Flavored Bitters

BAR TOOLS

Sometimes mixing a drink is as simple as pouring the ingredients. Other times, you need to do a little more. Bar tools are there to make your life a bit easier when it comes to mixing up these more complicated cocktails. From the cocktail shaker to the muddler, these are the tools that you should be sure to have in your home bar.

Must-Haves

Cocktail shaker

Strainer

Jigger

Knife

Bottle opener

Corkscrew

Nice to Have

Cocktail stirrer

Muddler

Juicer

Zester

GLASSWARE

Must-Haves

Pint Glass

Shot Glass

Old Fashioned Glass

Highball Glass

Nice to Have

Margarita Glass

Cocktail Glass

Champagne Flute

Wish List

Hurricane Glass

Daiquiri Glass

Irish Coffee Glass

Mason Jar

Sour Glass

PARTY MIXERS

If you're having a party, you'll want to have a few of these on hand for easy mixing! Even if you aren't looking to mix up specific cocktails, these mixers go great with most types of alcohol and will keep most party guests happy.

Coca-Cola	Tonic Water	Maraschino Cherries
Sprite	Club Soda	Oranges
Ginger Ale	Ice	Mint
Cranberry Juice	Lemons	
Fruit Punch	Limes	

VODKA

If there's one type of liquor that people tend to have lying around the house more than any other, it's probably vodka. And why not? Vodka can be mixed with just about anything. Its taste isn't particularly assertive, and it can take on the flavor of just about anything, contributing a healthy bite of alcohol into any otherwise unexciting drink.

The idea behind *The Home Bartender* is that cocktails don't have to be complicated. They don't have to have a hundred different flavors vying for the attention of your palate. In fact, most cocktails don't call for more than four ingredients. And sometimes the very best cocktails are the ones put together from whatever you happened to have lying around. So, what better to lead off with than vodka?

In the following pages, you'll find recipes both old and new, familiar and unfamiliar, with a new spin on some classic tastes and a variety of different ways to inject a little boozy goodness into a simple mix of flavors. Vodka cocktails are simple, fresh, and, above all, adaptable. You're sure to find something you like, so give it a try!

LONG ISLAND EXPRESS

The Long Island Iced Tea is one of the most popular (and strong) cocktails on the planet earth, but it has far more than four ingredients (in fact, it has more than four different *liquors* alone). Still, the spirit of the cocktail should live on, and it does just that in the Long Island Express. Trimming some of the fat (not *literal* fat—that would be disgusting) from the original recipe, we are left with a simple vodka and cola recipe, with a few extra ingredients to ensure that you won't want for flavor.

BASIC INGREDIENTS

 1/2 lemon (juiced)

 1 part vodka

 1 splash triple sec

 2 parts cola

 1 lemon slice (garnish)

GLASSWARE:
Highball glass.

1. Juice the lemon over ice, then add the vodka and a splash of triple sec.

2. Add cola to fill, then stir until thoroughly mixed.

3. Garnish with a slice of lemon and enjoy!

VARIATION. The Long Island Iced Tea traditionally contains vodka, rum, tequila, and gin. If you think it sounds better to make the Long Island Express with any of the other liquors rather than vodka, the flavors should hold up well regardless of which liquor you choose to use as a base.

NON ISLAND ICED TEA

While the traditional Long Island Iced Tea is built around many different types of alcohol, the Non Island Iced Tea is a combination of a variety of different refreshing beverages. On their own, iced tea, lemonade, and cola are delicious. Together, they make something a little bit more. Unusual? Sure. But why not go out on a limb once in a while?

BASIC INGREDIENTS

 I part iced tea (unsweetened)

 I part lemonade

 I part cola

 I lemon wedge (garnish)

 GLASSWARE: Highball glass.

1. Add the ingredients together in your glass. Stir until mixed.

2. Garnish with a lemon wedge and enjoy!

CAPESCREW

Two of the most famous vodka cocktails are the Screwdriver, traditionally consisting of vodka and orange juice, and the Cape Cod, made with vodka and cranberry juice. Well, as any seasoned breakfaster will surely tell you, few flavors go together quite as well as orange juice and cranberry juice. Mixed together, they create a flavor combination of sweet and tart that can tantalize any palate. Add in a little vodka and triple sec, and you've got the Capescrew, a combination of two favorites that takes both to the next level.

BASIC INGREDIENTS

 I part vodka

 I splash triple sec

 I part orange juice

 I part cranberry juice

 I orange wheel (garnish)

 GLASSWARE:
Highball glass.

1. Pour the vodka over ice and add a splash of triple sec.

2. Add the orange juice and cranberry juice and stir until thoroughly mixed.

3. Garnish with an orange wheel and enjoy!

VARIATIONS

- For more fruity flavor, try orange vodka or cranberry vodka instead of unflavored vodka. Or play with the ratios to get just the right mix of flavor you prefer.
- The Capescrew is similar to the Sex on the Beach, which features slightly different ratios and peach schnapps in place of triple sec. Give that one a whirl!

SEA BREEZE

A traditional vodka cocktail, the Sea Breeze plays with a variety of different citrus flavors to create a sweet concoction perfect for relaxing with on the beach on a hot summer day. Grapefruit, cranberry, and lime juice bounce off one another as the drink reaches your tongue, providing a cool, crisp, and refreshing counterbalance to the sun's rays beating down on you.

BASIC INGREDIENTS

 1/2 lime (juiced)

 1 part vodka

 2 parts cranberry juice

 1 part grapefruit juice

 1 lime wheel (garnish)

 Cherry (garnish)

GLASSWARE:
Highball glass.

1. Juice half a lime over ice, then add vodka.

2. Add cranberry juice and grapefruit juice and stir until thoroughly mixed.

3. Garnish with a lime wheel—and maybe even a cherry—and enjoy!

DON'T HAVE FRESH LEMONS OR LIMES?

Don't fret! You can always use lemon or lime juice from the store. The average lemon contains about 3 tablespoons of juice, while the average lime contains about 2 tablespoons. If your drink calls for the juice of ½ lime, you can easily deduce that they're asking for 1 tablespoon of lime juice.

BLASTOFF

Vodka cocktails are great, but sometimes you don't need an entire glass to get the job done. Shots can be a tricky thing, but when they're good, they're very good. It takes a certain amount of skill to impart enough flavor into that one gulp to make you say "that was great!" Such is the case with the blastoff cocktail, one swallow of which will pucker your mouth and electrify your palate.

BASIC INGREDIENTS

1 oz vodka

1/2 oz grapefruit juice

1 squeeze lemon juice

1 squeeze lime juice

GLASSWARE:
Shot glass.

1. Pour the vodka and grapefruit juice into a shot glass and finish with a quick squeeze of lemon and lime juice.

2. Toss it back and enjoy!

WHITE RUSSIAN

What could be better than a White Russian? This simple mixture of vodka, coffee liqueur, and cream provides a rich, delicious, and refreshing flavor perfect for summer and winter alike!

BASIC INGREDIENTS

1 part vodka

1 part coffee liqueur

2 parts cream

GLASSWARE:

Old Fashioned glass.

1. Fill an Old Fashioned glass with ice and add the vodka and coffee liqueur.

2. Slowly pour the cream over the vodka mixture.

3. Stir the ingredients together slowly and enjoy!

Some prefer to keep the cream and the liquor as separated as possible, even when drinking. This is up to the preference of the drinker, but you may find that the bottom of the drink is difficult to drink without the addition of the cream. By mixing them together, you'll get a nice, rich, golden color in your glass.

THE DIRTY SPY

The Vodka Martini is, of course, the drink that James Bond made famous, though it was already one of the most popular drinks in the world long before 007 put in his first order. Martini drinkers will know that the famous spy's request for his cocktail to be "shaken, not stirred" was an unusual one, as the Martini is not typically prepared this way. In honor of this unusual request, the Dirty Spy is a simple Dirty Martini prepared in a cocktail shaker.

BASIC INGREDIENTS

 3 parts vodka

 1 part dry vermouth

 1 splash green olive brine

 1 pimento-stuffed green olive

 GLASSWARE:
Cocktail glass.

1. Add the vodka, vermouth, and olive brine to a cocktail shaker filled with ice. Shake well.

2. Strain the resulting mixture into a Cocktail glass and add a cocktail olive (or a couple). Enjoy!

VARIATIONS

- While the Dirty Spy makes use of cocktail olives and olive brine, a traditional martini simply uses lemon juice, with a bit of lemon rind as a garnish.
- The original Martini was made with gin, so if you find the taste of juniper more to your liking, you can always try that!

CREAMSICLE

If you're like me, chances are you grew up eating Creamsicle popsicles, and this drink captures that flavor. This delicious combination of orange and cream will sweep you straight back to your childhood on a wave of nostalgia—with an adult twist.

BASIC INGREDIENTS

 I part orange juice

 I part vodka

 I part cream

 I splash triple sec

 I orange slice (garnish)

GLASSWARE:
 Old Fashioned glass.

1. Stir the ingredients together in a mixing glass.

2. Strain the resulting mixture over ice.

3. Garnish with an orange slice and enjoy!

VARIATION. As always, the ratios can be adjusted until you find a drink that you suits you. Mixology may have become an increasingly popular skill, but it's far from an exact science. The purpose of every cocktail is for the drinker to enjoy it, and that should always be your end goal.

STRAWBERRIES AND CREAM

The Creamsicle is a delicious drink, but the orange isn't the only fruit known to pair well with cream. Enter the Strawberries and Cream cocktail, combining vanilla and strawberry vodka with some rich cream to create a tasty, filling, and—thanks to the grenadine—colorful cocktail sure to delight.

BASIC INGREDIENTS

1 part strawberry vodka

1 part vanilla vodka

2 parts cream

1 splash grenadine

1 fresh strawberry (garnish)

GLASSWARE:
Old Fashioned glass.

1. Pour the strawberry vodka and vanilla vodka over ice. Top with cream and stir until thoroughly mixed.

2. Finish with a splash of grenadine for color. Garnish with a fresh strawberry and enjoy!

WHAT'S THE DIFFERENCE BETWEEN A DASH AND A SPLASH? They're definitely inexact measurements, but a dash is a tiny addition, just enough to impart a little flavor. A splash is a bit bigger—essentially just a quick pour into the drink. If you feel the need for an exact measurement, you can use a teaspoon and a tablespoon.

MINT MULE

6 mint leaves

1 lime wedge (juiced)

1 part vodka

2 parts ginger beer

1 lime wheel (garnish)

Turn the page for the recipe!

⟶

MINT MULE

The Moscow Mule is a popular vodka cocktail featuring primarily vodka and ginger beer. The sharpness of each of those flavors make this a winning combination, but sometimes it can be a bit much. The Moscow Mule is typically tempered with a bit of lime juice, but let's further take it down by adding a bit of mint to the party as well.

BASIC INGREDIENTS

 6 mint leaves

 1 lime wedge (juiced)

 1 part vodka

 2 parts ginger beer

 1 lime wheel (garnish)

GLASSWARE:
Highball glass
(or copper mug).

1. Tear the mint leaves in half to release the flavor, then add them to the bottom of the glass.

2. Add the juice from the lime wedge and muddle the mint leaves. Add ice.

3. Pour in the vodka and ginger beer. Stir until thoroughly mixed.

4. Garnish with a lime wheel and enjoy!

HOW DO YOU MUDDLE INGREDIENTS? It's easy. Simply put them at the bottom of your glass and use a blunt instrument to lightly mash them together. You can use a muddler, but if you don't have one, the back of a spoon will work just fine.

VIRGIN MULE

The Virgin Mule is a delicious and refreshing alternative to its boozy namesake, and you can drink as many of them as you please!

BASIC INGREDIENTS

 1/2 lime (juiced)

 8 oz ginger beer

 Lime slice (garnish)

 GLASSWARE:
Highball glass
(or copper mule).

1. Juice the lime into your glass, then add ice.

2. Add ginger beer to fill, then garnish with a slice of lime. Enjoy!

RING #4

You know what's better than three? Four. The Ring #4 combines a splash of four different fruit flavors into an inviting mix sure to make you feel like a champion. The grenadine adds a gorgeous red coloration that makes this drink feel like a throwback to summer days spent sitting on the porch drinking a refreshing glass of raspberry lemonade. Whether you're downing these in August or February, the tasty combination of fruit flavors is sure to have you coming back for two, three, or even twelve.

BASIC INGREDIENTS

 1 part raspberry vodka

 1 splash triple sec

 2 parts lemonade

 1 splash grenadine

 lemon wheel (garnish)

GLASSWARE:
Highball glass.

1. Add ice to a highball glass and add the vodka and triple sec.

2. Fill the rest of the glass with lemonade and top with a splash of grenadine to add an inviting red hue to the drink.

3. Garnish with a lemon wheel and enjoy.

> If there are four things that every home bar should have (outside of the standard categories of alcohol), they are vermouth (sweet and dry), bitters, grenadine, and triple sec. These ingredients are called for in small amounts in hundreds of cocktails, and can be used to spice up a wide variety of different drinks.

CLASSIC
COSMOPOLITAN

2 parts Skyy Vodka

1 part triple sec

1 part cranberry juice

1 splash lime juice

1 lime wheel (garnish)

Turn the page for the recipe!
→

CLASSIC COSMOPOLITAN

Known for being fruity, delicious, and, well, *pink*, the Cosmopolitan is one of the tastiest and most popular vodka drinks around. Oddly, men tend to shy away from ordering the Cosmopolitan. It's a shame, really. It's the same color as a Cape Cod or a Greyhound, and it's served in more or less the same way as a Martini. Regardless, the Cosmopolitan is a delicious, sweet, and fruity drink perfect for a night out on the town or a cozy night in the apartment.

BASIC INGREDIENTS

 2 parts Skyy Vodka

 I part triple sec

 I part cranberry juice

 I splash lime juice

 I lime wheel (garnish)

 GLASSWARE:
Cocktail glass.

1. Fill a cocktail shaker with ice and add the liquid ingredients. Shake well.

2. Strain the resulting mixture into a Cocktail glass and garnish with a lime wheel. Enjoy!

PERFECT COSMOPOLITAN

If you're drinking a classic cocktail like the Cosmopolitan, why not go all the way with it? Use only the finest ingredients and you might be surprised to discover that this already delicious treat can actually get even tastier. Make sure you're using the freshest ingredients, too—that means fresh squeezed limes only!

BASIC INGREDIENTS

 2 parts Grey Goose Vodka

 I part triple sec

 I part cranberry juice

 I lime wedge (juiced)

 I lime wheel (garnish)

GLASSWARE:
Cocktail glass.

1. Fill a cocktail shaker with ice and add the vodka, triple sec, cranberry juice, and lime juice (squeeze the lime straight in). Shake well.

2. Strain the resulting mixture into a Cocktail glass and garnish with a lime wheel. Enjoy!

BUDGET COSMOPOLITAN

Then again, why go over the top for a cocktail that's really little more than a mixture of three different fruit flavors, with a splash of vodka thrown in for good measure? If that's your mentality, then maybe the Budget Cosmo is for you. Never mind the garnishes and who needs fresh limes? Grab the vodka you've got on the shelf, mix it up until it's nice and pink, and presto! Deliciousness.

BASIC INGREDIENTS

2 parts Svedka Vodka

1 part triple sec

1 part cranberry juice

1 splash lime juice

GLASSWARE:
Cocktail glass.

1. Fill a cocktail shaker with ice and add the vodka, triple sec, cranberry juice, and lime juice. Shake well.

2. Strain the resulting mixture into a Cocktail glass and garnish with a lime wheel. Enjoy!

VIRGIN COSMOPOLITAN

Forget the booze and rock out this summer with the Virgin Cosmopolitan, a classy and colorful way to keep cool while remaining sober. The Virgin Cosmopolitan combines the delicious flavors that you'll find in any standard Cosmopolitan and gives them a splash of fizz while passing on the vodka. It's a surprisingly good way to spice up a sober evening and is the perfect drink for any designated driver.

BASIC INGREDIENTS

 4 parts cranberry juice

 I lime wedge (juiced)

 I part Sprite

 I lime wheel (garnish)

 GLASSWARE:
Cocktail glass.

1. Add the cranberry juice to a Cocktail glass and squeeze in the juice from one lime wedge.

2. Top with a splash of Sprite.

3. Garnish with a lime wheel and enjoy!

BETTY'S COSMO

If you love Cosmos and want to try something a little bit different from the standard fare, give Betty's Cosmo a try. With equal parts vodka and cranberry juice cocktail and a tantalizing mixture of fresh lime juice and its sweetened counterpart, Betty's Cosmo is a delicious drink perfect for serving at family gatherings or sipping on the back porch.

BASIC INGREDIENTS

 3 oz Skyy vodka

 3 oz cranberry juice cocktail

 1 oz Cointreau

 1 dash Rose's Lime Juice

 1 squeeze fresh lime

 GLASSWARE:
Cocktail glass.

1. Add the vodka, cranberry juice cocktail, Cointreau, and Rose's Lime Juice to a cocktail shaker filled with ice. Shake well.

2. Strain the resulting mixture into a cocktail glass.

3. Top with a squeeze of fresh lime and enjoy!

PEACH TREE ICED TEA

What's better than a little peach iced tea on a summer day? Iced tea is one of the most refreshing drinks on the planet, so adding a little vodka to the mix can't go awry. And where better to get that peach flavor that makes you feel all warm and fuzzy than by adding a little peach schnapps? Peach Tree Iced Tea is a drink that towers over other iced tea cocktails. Is it the best one out there? You be the judge.

BASIC INGREDIENTS

 6 mint leaves

 1 part peach schnapps

 1 part vodka

 2 parts iced tea

 GLASSWARE:
Highball glass.

1. Tear the mint leaves in half and add them to the bottom of your glass. Add the peach schnapps and muddle together.

2. Add ice to the glass, then pour in the vodka and iced tea. Stir until thoroughly mixed and enjoy!

42

LIQUID APPLE PIE

1 part vanilla vodka

1 dash brown sugar

3 parts apple cider

1 dash cinnamon

1 cinnamon stick (garnish)

Turn the page for the recipe!

LIQUID APPLE PIE

This drink captures what you love most about the flavor of homemade apple pie and puts it in a glass instead of on a plate. In fact, the drink tastes so good that you might not even realize how strong it is. Much like when eating mom's apple pie, moderation is key!

BASIC INGREDIENTS

 1 part vanilla vodka

 1 dash brown sugar

 3 parts apple cider

 1 dash cinnamon

 1 cinnamon stick (garnish)

 GLASSWARE:
Mason jar
or glass mug.

1. Add the vanilla vodka and brown sugar to your glass and stir them together.

2. Pour the apple cider over top and finish with a dusting of cinnamon.

3. Garnish with a cinnamon stick and enjoy!

VARIATIONS

- While you can drink it cold, the drink is (in my humble opinion) considerably better when served warm.
- If you're feeling particularly festive, garnish with a star anise.

VIRGIN
APPLE PIE

Virgin Apple Pie is another liquid way to evoke memories of crisp, cool, fall evenings—but without worrying about a hangover in the morning.

BASIC INGREDIENTS

3 parts apple cider

I part cream soda

I dash cinnamon

I dollop whipped cream (garnish)

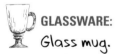
GLASSWARE:
Glass mug.

1. Add the apple cider and cream soda to your glass.

2. Top with a dash of cinnamon, then stir until thoroughly mixed.

3. Add a dollop of whipped cream if you wish and enjoy!

CHERRY LIME SPIKE

Cherry and lime have traditionally gone well together, but rather than drink a regular old glass of cherry limeade, why not spike it with a little vodka? A little cherry vodka can go a long way, both in terms of adding alcohol to the cocktail and adding flavor.

BASIC INGREDIENTS

 I part cherry vodka

 I part lime juice

 2 parts club soda

 I dash grenadine

 I lime wheel (garnish)

 GLASSWARE:
Highball glass.

1. Pour the cherry vodka and lime juice into your glass and stir together. Add ice.

2. Add club soda to fill, then top with a small dash of grenadine for color.

3. Garnish with a lime wheel and enjoy!

VARIATION. Use limeade or lime-flavored club soda instead of lime juice.

THE ESSENTIAL BLOODY MARY

I dash Worcestershire sauce

I dash lemon juice

I part vodka

2 parts tomato juice

Garnish with anything your heart desires

Turn the page for the recipe!

THE ESSENTIAL BLOODY MARY

The Essential Bloody Mary takes the Bloody Mary and distills (no pun intended) it down to its most essential ingredients for your mixing pleasure.

BASIC INGREDIENTS

 1 dash Worcestershire sauce

 1 dash lemon juice

 1 part vodka

 2 parts tomato juice

 Garnish with anything your heart desires

 GLASSWARE:
Pint glass.

1. Add the Worcestershire sauce and lemon juice to a pint glass, then add ice.

2. Pour in the vodka and tomato juice and stir until thoroughly mixed.

3. Garnish with bacon, olives, lemon wedges, celery, pickles, an entire hamburger, or anything else your heart desires and enjoy!

The Bloody Mary is a simple drink, but it's made complicated by the fact that everyone has come to expect increasingly outrageous garnishes. From a simple rasher of bacon to an entire bacon cheeseburger, the garnishes for this traditional drink have gotten out of control. This isn't a bad thing—now you can add whatever you like to your Bloody Mary without fear of strange looks from anyone!

VIRGIN MARY

A Bloody Mary is tasty, but then so is regular old tomato juice. Spice up your tomato juice with a few of the fixings that the Bloody Mary is famous for, giving you a great new drink with which to greet the day!

BASIC INGREDIENTS

 8 oz tomato juice

 I dash Worcestershire sauce

 I dash lemon juice

 I dash pepper

 Garnish with anything your heart desires

 GLASSWARE: Pint glass.

1. Add ice to your glass, then fill with tomato juice.

2. Add a dash of Worcestershire sauce, lemon juice, and black pepper. Stir thoroughly

3. Garnish with anything you please!

VARIATION. This is just the base for a successful Virgin Mary. If you'd like to add other common ingredients (like horseradish or salt, for example) that you happen to have lying around, you can easily build off this!

VODKA SUNRISE

As beautiful as it is traditional, the Vodka Sunrise is a drink popular both for its tasty flavor and gorgeous hues. Its appearance lives up to its name—the cocktail looks like nothing so much as the sun rising over the horizon in the morning, with reds, oranges, and yellows playing off one another in a fantastic medley of color.

BASIC INGREDIENTS

1 part vodka

1 dash lemon juice

2 parts orange juice

1 splash grenadine

1 maraschino cherry (garnish)

1 orange slice (garnish)

GLASSWARE:
Highball glass.

1. Add ice to a glass and pour in the vodka and lemon juice. Mix together.

2. Add orange juice to fill, then top with a splash of grenadine. Rather than stirring, allow the grenadine to slowly filter down through the orange juice and vodka.

3. Garnish with a maraschino cherry and an orange slice and enjoy!

VARIATIONS

■ Variations involve adding different regional flavors, such as the Tropical Sunrise (made with pineapple juice) or the Mango Sunrise (made with mango juice). You can always play around by adding different flavors until you find something you like.

■ The Tequila Sunrise is perhaps even more popular than the Vodka Sunrise and can be made (predictably) by substituting tequila in place of vodka (see page 179).

■ For a Virgin Sunrise, see page 181.

PEAR PRESSURE

We use the word "vanilla" as a code word for bland, but that isn't quite right. It's more of a subtle flavor than, say, chocolate, but that's part of what makes it great. It's definitely what makes vanilla vodka great and one of the reasons that vanilla vodka and pear go together so well. Subtlety of flavor is what separates pear from other fruits, and adding it together with vanilla makes for an understated drink you're sure to love.

BASIC INGREDIENTS

I part vanilla vodka

I part pear juice

I splash lime juice

Sugar (for rimming)

I pear slice, thinly cut (garnish)

GLASSWARE:
Old Fashioned glass.

1. Add the liquid ingredients to a cocktail shaker filled with ice and shake well.

2. Rim an Old Fashioned glass with sugar and strain the cocktail shaker into it.

3. Garnish with a thinly sliced pear and enjoy!

NEVER USED SUGAR OR SALT TO RIM THE EDGE OF A GLASS BEFORE?

It's easy. Although water will work just fine to make the sugar stick, you can add a little extra flavor by rubbing the edge of a lemon or lime along the rim of your glass instead. Then simply turn the glass over and press the rim into a bowl of sugar, salt, or whatever else you might be rimming the glass with. Presto! Added flavor and beautiful presentation.

DRINK THE C

C is for Cointreau, that's good enough for me. But it helps to have a few more flavors in there, like cherry vodka, coconut rum, and cola, to round out the flavor profile of this C-heavy concoction. Is it a bit contrived for the sake of its name? Maybe. But it's also a delicious combination of flavors with a simple cola base, making this a simple, straightforward, and tasty cocktail for any time.

BASIC INGREDIENTS

 1 part cherry vodka

2 parts cola

 1 splash coconut rum

1 splash Cointreau

 1 cocktail cherry (garnish)

1. Add the cherry vodka and cola to your glass and stir together.

2. Top with a splash of coconut rum and Cointreau and stir again.

3. Garnish with a cocktail cherry and enjoy!

GLASSWARE:
Old Fashioned glass.

MOCHA MOCHA MOCHA

Beware: This is a drink as dangerous as any out there. It is a mixture of sweet flavors so delicious that you're likely to forget that you're drinking something extremely strong. With three out of four ingredients containing alcohol, it's the sort of drink that might put you on the floor before you realize what's happened. Still, if flavor is what's most important (and I maintain that it is!), you won't do much better than this fantastic concoction.

BASIC INGREDIENTS

 I part vodka

 I part chocolate liqueur

 I part coffee liqueur

 2 parts milk

GLASSWARE:
Old Fashioned glass.

1. Add the vodka, liqueurs, and milk to a cocktail shaker filled with ice and shake vigorously.

2. Strain the resulting mixture into an Old Fashioned glass filled with ice and enjoy!

GINGER BINGER

1 part vodka

1 splash triple sec

1 part grapefruit juice

2 parts ginger ale

1 lime wheel (garnish)

1 sprig mint (garnish)

Turn the page for the recipe!

GINGER BINGER

Ginger goes well with vodka, and while ginger beer is always a popular cocktail ingredient, ginger ale has none of the harsh bite that ginger beer all too often imparts to cocktails. Ginger ale, a subtle background flavor upon which to build, allows other flavors to come to the forefront and contribute to the cocktail's flavor profile in ways they would be otherwise unable. The Ginger Binger makes use of this with a little orange and grapefruit flavor springing to the forefront.

BASIC INGREDIENTS

I part vodka

I splash triple sec

I part grapefruit juice

2 parts ginger ale

I lime wheel (garnish)

I sprig mint (garnish)

GLASSWARE:
Highball glass.

1. Fill a highball glass with ice and add the vodka, triple sec, and grapefruit juice. Stir together.

2. Top with ginger ale and stir again. Garnish with a lime wheel—and maybe even a sprig of mint—and enjoy!

RUM

A more assertive flavor than vodka, rum tends to spring to the forefront of any drink it finds itself in. This is not a bad thing—the distinctive flavor of rum is something to build around rather than cover up. Some of the most famous rum cocktails are simply too complex to be included in a book of simple recipes. But maybe this is a blessing in disguise, forcing even the most seasoned rum drinker to step outside his or her comfort zone.

The Home Bartender is about making things easy on all of us. Why go to the store to gather the ingredients for something crazily complex when you can make a dozen simple cocktails with ingredients you probably already have? Whether it's the simple addition of a splash of grenadine in the Roses for Alex cocktail or the slightly more refined palate of the Daiquiri Twist, even the simplest rum drinks can offer a depth of flavor that other cocktails just can't match. Bust out the lime juice, check the pantry for sugar, and get ready for simple flavors everyone will love.

DAIQUIRI TWIST

This take on the classic Daiquiri recipe substitutes a bit of triple sec for some of the white rum, taking down the intensity of the alcohol in favor of a more flavorful, easily drinkable cocktail. The Daiquiri Twist really lets the flavor of the rum shine without overwhelming your tongue with an overpowering taste of booze.

BASIC INGREDIENTS

 2 parts white rum

 I part lime juice

 I part triple sec

 I splash simple syrup

 I lime wheel (garnish)

GLASSWARE:
Cocktail glass.

1. Fill a cocktail shaker with ice and add the liquid ingredients. Shake well.

2. Strain the resulting mixture into a Cocktail glass.

3. Garnish with a lime wheel. Enjoy!

VARIATION. Everyone on earth has heard of the **Strawberry Daiquiri**, and you can make one by just adding a bit of strawberry schnapps in place of the triple sec. If you want the frozen version of the drink, add about half a cup of ice and blend it all together.

DON'T HAVE SIMPLE SYRUP? It's surprisingly easy to make. Simply add sugar and water to a pot in a 1:1 ratio, then bring it to a boil. When the cloudy mixture becomes completely clear, it's ready!

CUBA LIBRE

Another classic rum cocktail, the Cuba Libre is really little more than a standard rum and cola with a twist of lime and mint. That's not a negative—many of the best cocktails are the ones with simplest flavors. Why spend any more time than you have to mixing a drink, and why pretend that you need complex flavors to be tasty? The Cuba Libre is the perfect answer the complicated drinks favored by so many mixologists. No need to show off here. Flavor is all you need.

BASIC INGREDIENTS

 6 mint leaves

 1/2 lime (juiced)

 1 part white rum

 2 parts cola

 1 lime wedge (garnish)

GLASSWARE:
Highball glass.

1. Tear the mint leaves in half and add them to the bottom of the glass. Add the lime juice and muddle together.

2. Add ice to the glass and pour in the rum and cola. Stir until thoroughly mixed.

3. Garnish with a lime wedge and enjoy!

TROPICAL STORM

The Tropical Storm scales back the ever-popular Hurricane recipe into something a little more manageable for everyday consumption. After all, who keeps three types of rum on hand? The Tropical Storm maintains the flavors that make the Hurricane so beloved while decreasing the complexity and creating something that you can easily make at home.

BASIC INGREDIENTS

 I part white rum

 I part dark rum

 I part passion fruit syrup

 1/2 lemon (juiced)

I maraschino cherry (garnish)

GLASSWARE:
Hurricane glass.

1. Add the liquid ingredients to a cocktail shaker filled with ice and shake vigorously.

2. Strain the resulting mixture into a Hurricane glass.

3. Garnish with a maraschino cherry and enjoy!

VARIATION. Part of what makes the **Hurricane** so popular is the inclusion of high-proof rum, which has been dropped in the slightly weaker Tropical Storm (get it?). If you really want that extra bit of boozy goodness in the drink, sub in some high-proof rum in place of the white rum.

SUNBURST

One of the great things about coconut rum is that its understated flavor doesn't force itself into the forefront quite as much as regular rum, allowing you to play off its subtler flavor a bit more. It's also quite tasty in its own right. The Sunburst takes full advantage of this, mixing it with a few other tropical flavors to create a delicious burst of citrus with every sip.

BASIC INGREDIENTS

I part coconut rum

I part pineapple juice

I lemon wedge (juiced)

2 parts grapefruit juice

I grapefruit twist (garnish)

GLASSWARE:
Highball glass.

1. Add ice to your glass and add in the coconut rum, pineapple juice, and squeeze of lemon juice.

2. Top off with grapefruit juice and garnish with a grapefruit twist. Enjoy!

If you find yourself unable to make a perfect citrus twist, you can always just use a simple strip of zest. There are tools you can purchase to make it easier to create proper twists if you're married to the idea, though!

YOUR TAI

A scaled-back version of the Mai Tai, Your Tai keeps most of the flavors that make the Mai Tai great while making it a little easier to mix at home. Eschewing the usual Orgeat syrup, the drink still combines differing rum flavors with curacao and lime juice to make a cocktail that is startlingly strong considering how easy it is to drink.

BASIC INGREDIENTS

 2 parts white rum

 1 part dark rum

 1 part curacao

 1/2 lime (juiced)

 1 pineapple wedge (garnish)

 1 maraschino cherry (garnish)

GLASSWARE:
 Highball glass.

1. Add the rums, curacao, and lime juice to a cocktail shaker filled with ice and shake well.

2. Strain the resulting mixture into a Highball glass over ice.

3. Garnish with a pineapple wedge and a maraschino cherry and enjoy!

PIÑA COLADA

1 part white rum

1 part coconut milk

1 part triple sec

2 parts pineapple juice

Crushed ice (for blending)

1 pineapple wedge (garnish)

Turn the page for the recipe!

⟶

PIÑA COLADA

The Piña Colada is one of the most distinctive flavors you'll find in any cocktail. The coconut and pineapple combination might seem like an obvious one, but nobody has been able to replicate it quite as successfully as the tropical delight that is the Piña Colada. It's a fresh, creamy cocktail that's actually deceptively simple. For the speedy mixologist, we've added one ingredient—triple sec—to add an extra pop of freshness and keep the drink light!

BASIC INGREDIENTS

 I part white rum

 I part coconut milk

 I part triple sec

 2 parts pineapple juice

 Crushed ice (for blending)

 I pineapple wedge (garnish)

GLASSWARE:
Hurricane glass.

1. Add the white rum, coconut milk, triple sec, and pineapple juice to a blender with about ½ cup of ice. Blend until smooth.

2. Pour the resulting mixture into your glass and garnish with a pineapple wedge. Enjoy!

VIRGIN PIÑA COLADA

Piña Coladas are great, but too many of them can leave you on the ground wondering what happened. Why not opt for the non-alcoholic option, containing the same great coconut and pineapple taste with none of the head-ringing aftereffects? The Virgin Piña Colada is a delicious, slushy drink guaranteed to leave you wanting more. Makes 4 servings.

BASIC INGREDIENTS

 I part coconut cream

 3 parts pineapple juice

 2 cup to 4 cups crushed ice

 4 pineapple wedges (garnish)

 4 maraschino cherries (garnish)

GLASSWARE:
Hurricane glass.

1. Add coconut cream, pineapple juice, and ice to the blender and blend until smooth. Add as much ice as you want until you reach your desired consistency. It doesn't need to be too thick; when the ice melts, you don't want to leave yourself with a watered-down drink.

2. Pour into individual Hurricane glasses, garnish with pineapple wedges and cherries, and enjoy!

BANANA CREAM PIE

Vodka might pair well with cream, but rum pairs well with tropical fruits like the coconut and banana. There's just something about the flavor of rum that screams "beach." So why not blend up some bananas and cream for a thick, refreshing, smoothie-like drink that packs a hefty punch of alcohol? The Banana Cream Pie is a unique and unusual cocktail that you're sure to love.

BASIC INGREDIENTS

 1 banana (pureed)

 1 part vanilla rum

 1 part banana rum

 1 part cream

 1 dusting nutmeg (garnish)

 1 banana circle (garnish)

 GLASSWARE:
Highball glass.

1. Cut one circle off the banana to reserve for a garnish.

2. Put the rest of the banana, vanilla rum, banana rum, and cream in a blender and blend until smooth.

3. Pour the resulting mixture into a Highball glass and dust with a bit of nutmeg. Garnish with the banana circle and enjoy!

CARIBBEAN
CRANBERRY TWIST

While rum is certainly tropical enough on its own, coconut rum can still help push any cocktail to the next level when it comes to Caribbean flavors. Enter the Caribbean Cranberry Twist, which makes use of the boozy goodness of coconut rum and triple sec while accenting those flavors with orange juice and cranberry juice. These light, fresh flavors will transport you straight to be beach no matter where you might be.

BASIC INGREDIENTS

 I part coconut rum

 I part orange juice

 I part cranberry juice

 I splash triple sec

 I orange slice (garnish)

GLASSWARE:
Highball glass.

1. Fill a Highball glass with ice and add the rum, orange juice, and cranberry juice. Stir until thoroughly mixed.

2. Finish with a splash of triple sec and garnish with an orange slice. Enjoy!

RED RUM FIZZ

All of these rum drinks made with fruit juices and liqueurs are tasty, but they can get a little heavy after a while. Break it up by adding a little fizz to your life with the Red Rum Fizz. Heavy on the orange flavor, with a velvety red color thanks to the grenadine, the Red Rum Fizz is as beautiful as it is airy and delicious.

BASIC INGREDIENTS

 I part rum

 I part orange juice

 I part club soda

 I splash grenadine

 I maraschino cherry (garnish)

 GLASSWARE:
Highball glass.

1. Mix the rum and orange juice together in a Highball glass with ice.

2. Add club soda to fill.

3. Finish with a splash of grenadine and garnish with a maraschino cherry. Enjoy!

ONE DARK NIGHT

Ginger beer is a great ingredient to use in a huge number of cocktails, but tempering that harsh bite can be a bit of a challenge. Enter Orgeat syrup, a delightfully almondy ingredient that adds a bit of nutty creaminess to any drink. With a bit of lime juice to elevate the drink with a bit of citrus, One Stormy Night is perfect for any night, stormy or otherwise.

BASIC INGREDIENTS

 I part dark rum

 2 parts ginger beer

 1/2 lime (juiced)

 I splash Orgeat syrup

 I lime slice (garnish)

 GLASSWARE:
Highball glass.

1. Add ice to a Highball glass and pour in the rum, ginger beer, and lime juice. Stir until thoroughly mixed.

2. Finish with a splash of Orgeat syrup. Do not stir.

3. Garnish with a slice of lime and enjoy!

CIDERMEISTER

More coconut rum? Naturally! Jagermeister may have a reputation for being the chosen drink of college students everywhere, but anyone can enjoy this unique spiced liquor. When paired with a base of something a bit more subtle, like coconut rum, it can actually add quite a bit of flavor to any drink. Apple cider is best when spiced anyway, making it the perfect mixing agent for the delicious and unique Cidermeister drink.

BASIC INGREDIENTS

 I part coconut rum

 I part Jagermeister

 4 parts fresh apple cider

 I dusting cinnamon

 I cinnamon stick (garnish)

 GLASSWARE:
Highball glass.

1. Add ice to a Highball glass and pour in the coconut rum, Jagermeister, and apple cider. Stir until thoroughly mixed.

2. Finish with a dusting of cinnamon. Add a cinnamon stick for garnish and enjoy!

VANILLA FLOAT

Have you ever noticed that when you add spiced rum to cola, the result tastes a little bit like vanilla? Well, there is no reason not to take full advantage of that and make yourself a vanilla-heavy cocktail with a splash of ice cream to boot. It's so simple you'll be kicking yourself for not thinking of it before!

BASIC INGREDIENTS

 I part spiced rum

 2 parts cola

 I scoop vanilla ice cream

 GLASSWARE: Pint glass.

1. Pour the spiced rum and cola into a Pint glass.

2. Add a scoop of vanilla ice cream, and serve with a long spoon.

VARIATIONS. Ice cream floats can be made in many different ways, so feel free to choose any flavor combination you like. If you'd rather make it with root beer and coconut ice cream, go for it! You might even sub in orange soda if you're feeling particularly adventurous. For an added bit of sweetness, rim the glass with sugar so you'll have something extra to enjoy when you slurp down what's left.

SPICED TEA

What could be better than a glass of iced tea on a hot summer day? How about Spiced Tea? Spiking your iced tea with a splash of spiced rum and adding a bit of lemon and mint can go a long way toward developing the complex-but-simple flavors you deserve. Why settle for less when having more is so easy?

BASIC INGREDIENTS

 6 mint leaves

 1/2 lemon (juiced)

 1 part spiced rum

 2 parts iced tea

 1 lemon wheel (garnish)

 GLASSWARE:
Highball glass.

1. Tear the mint leaves in half and add them to the bottom of your glass. Add the lemon juice and muddle them together.

2. Add ice, then add the spiced rum and iced tea. Stir until thoroughly mixed.

3. Garnish with a lemon wheel and enjoy!

COOL SUMMER

20 mint leaves

4 lime wedges (juiced)

1 part white rum

2 parts lemonade

4 lemon wheels (garnish)

Turn the page for the recipe!

COOL SUMMER

The great thing about lemonade is how easy it is to mix with just about any liquor. Vodka, gin, rum... even whiskey mixes just fine with that greatest of all summer drinks. So add a little rum to your lemonade, add in a little extra citrus and lime flavor, and cool down with a refreshing Cool Summer cocktail. Make it by the pitcher and share with your friends! Makes 4 servings.

BASIC INGREDIENTS

 20 mint leaves

 4 lime wedges (juiced)

 1 part white rum

 2 parts lemonade

 4 lemon wheels (garnish)

GLASSWARE:
Highball glass.

1. Tear the mint leaves in half and add them to a pitcher. Juice the lime wedges into the pitcher and muddle the ingredients together as best you can.

2. Add ice, rum, and lemonade. Stir until thoroughly mixed.

3. Pour into individual glasses and garnish with lemon wheels! Enjoy!

AFTER DARK

The After Dark is essentially a pomegranate Italian soda with a dash of bitters and a healthy dose of rum, and doesn't that just sound fantastic? It's sweet and light, but also dark and bitter. It has a medley of different flavors that dance across your tongue, each contributing something just a little different to the drink.

BASIC INGREDIENTS

 1 part dark rum

 2 parts club soda

 1 splash pomegranate syrup

 2 drops bitters

 1 maraschino cherry (garnish)

 1 orange wedge

 GLASSWARE:
Old Fashioned glass.

1. Add ice to an Old Fashioned glass. Pour in the dark rum and top with club soda.

2. Add a splash of pomegranate syrup and let it settle into the club soda. Finish with two drops of bitters.

3. Garnish with a maraschino cherry and an orange wedge and enjoy!

ROSES FOR ALEX

Another drink on the lighter side of things, Roses for Alex plays the nice orange flavor of triple sec off a bit of white rum. The bright red color added by the grenadine will shine through, making you think of nothing so much as a dozen roses for someone you love.

BASIC INGREDIENTS

 I part white rum

 I part triple sec

 2 parts club soda

 I splash grenadine

 I maraschino cherry (garnish)

 GLASSWARE:
Old Fashioned glass.

1. Fill an Old Fashioned glass with ice, then add the white rum and triple sec. Top with club soda.

2. Finish with a splash of grenadine. Garnish with a maraschino cherry and enjoy!

FOUR FELLOWS

There are so many different kinds of rum, and some of them go quite well together. Many drinks make use of both white and dark rum, but how about the four most popular kinds of rum all together in one delicious shot? Whether shots are your thing or not, sometimes it's nice to combine a bunch of competing flavors together and just see what happens. The Four Fellows shot gives you one such occasion, and you might be surprised at just how easy it goes down.

BASIC INGREDIENTS

 I part white rum

 I part dark rum

 I part spiced rum

 I part coconut rum

GLASSWARE:
Shot glass.

1. Pour the four rums into a shot glass in roughly equal proportions. You can try to layer them if you like, but it will be a challenge.

2. Knock it back and enjoy!

VARIATION. If you want something a little stronger (you're a braver person than I), omit the coconut rum in favor of a high proof rum such as Bacardi 151. You'll lose some flavor, but it will definitely add a good deal of kick to an already strong drink.

CUBAN REDHEAD

1 part white rum

1 part coffee liqueur

1 part Irish cream

1 dash crème de menthe

1 mint sprig (garnish)

Turn the page for the recipe!

CUBAN REDHEAD

Rum and Irish cream aren't exactly a common mixture, but you might be surprised at how well they go together, especially with a bit of coffee liqueur to offset them. The addition of a dash of crème de menthe elevates this Irish-Cuban hybrid into something truly remarkable. Just watch your intake—this is a strong one.

BASIC INGREDIENTS

 I part white rum

 I part coffee liqueur

 I part Irish cream

 I dash crème de menthe

 I mint sprig (garnish)

GLASSWARE:
Old Fashioned glass.

1. Add the rum, coffee liqueur, and Irish cream to a cocktail shaker filled with ice. Shake vigorously.

2. Strain the resulting mixture into an Old Fashioned glass over ice. Top with a dash of crème de menthe.

3. Garnish with a mint sprig and enjoy!

CUBAN COFFEE

Irish Coffee is the famous mixture of Irish whiskey, coffee, and Irish cream, so it only makes sense that Cuban Coffee would feature Cuban rum. Cuban Coffee is a great cocktail for when you want to whisk away a hangover from the night before. With a helping of caffeine to keep you awake and a splash of booze to give you a buzz, it's hard to go wrong with this delicious cocktail.

BASIC INGREDIENTS

 I part dark Cuban rum

 3 parts coffee

 I spoonful sugar

 I splash cream liqueur

 GLASSWARE:
Irish Coffee glass.

1. Pour the rum and coffee into an Irish Coffee glass and stir together.

2. Add a spoonful of sugar and a dash of cream liqueur. Stir again until thoroughly mixed and enjoy!

PRIVATEER

1/2 lime (juiced)

1 part coconut rum

3 parts cola

1 lime wedge (garnish)

Turn the page for the recipe!

→

PRIVATEER

You don't need to do anything too fancy to maximize the deliciousness of coconut rum, and the Privateer proves it. With just a little coconut rum and lime, regular old cola becomes a culinary delight, dancing across your taste buds with a bubbly, fizzy airiness that packs a flavorful punch. Be bold and try something new!

BASIC INGREDIENTS

 1/2 lime (juiced)

 1 part coconut rum

 3 parts cola

 1 lime wedge (garnish)

 GLASSWARE:
Highball glass.

1. Squeeze the juice from ½ lime into your glass.

2. Add ice as desired, then add the rum and cola. Stir until mixed.

3. Garnish with a lime wedge and enjoy!

VIRGIN PRIVATEER

Lime and cola are good, but adding a little bit of coconut flavor is better. You've probably had coconut coffee or maybe even a coconut Italian soda, but the Virgin Privateer takes that great coconut flavor and uses it to accent lime and cola. The drink has a surprisingly complex flavor profile for something so easy to make, and you're sure to love it!

BASIC INGREDIENTS

 1/2 lime (juiced)

  1 oz coconut syrup

 8 oz cola

 1 lemon wheel (garnish)

GLASSWARE:
Highball glass.

1. Squeeze the juice from ½ of a lime into your glass.

2. Add ice, then add the coconut syrup and cola. Stir until mixed.

3. Garnish with a lemon wheel and enjoy!

ISLAND PUNCH

Here's a tasty drink that absolutely anyone can enjoy. A little Island Punch takes the distinct flavor of dark rum and pits it against sweet, tangy pineapple and orange juices to vie for your attention. A couple drops of bitters add a little bit of depth to this cocktail.

BASIC INGREDIENTS

 1 part dark rum

 1 part pineapple juice

 1 part orange juice

 2 drops bitters

 1 pineapple slice (garnish)

 GLASSWARE:
Pint glass.

1. Add the rum, juices, and bitters to a cocktail shaker filled with ice. Shake well.

2. Strain the resulting mixture into a pint glass over ice.

3. Garnish with a slice of pineapple and enjoy!

GIN

Ah, gin. The bite of alcohol combined with the freshness of juniper tastes like Christmas to me. Those who love gin tend to love the scent of pine, the clear crispness of the liquid, and how well it pairs with simple ingredients like club soda and lime. Gin is a great addition to a great many cocktails, but what makes it great is how well it can also stand on its own. The Gin Martini is one of the most famous gin drinks around, and most versions contain no more than two or three ingredients. After all, why muddle the taste of gin when it's already so delicious on its own? And let's not forget the Gin and Tonic (or its buffed up cousin, the 1505 G&T)—a drink so delicious that it needs naught but a hint of fizz and a taste of lemon to push it over the top.

Whereas harsher liquors like vodka tend to need extra ingredients to prop them up, gin cocktails are often remarkable in how well they complement the existing flavor of the gin. You should never feel the need to drown the flavor of gin, and this basic rule allows the principle behind *The Home Bartender* to shine. Nothing complex. Nothing over-the-top. Nothing that muddles a dozen different flavors until you can barely remember which liquor you started with. No, gin is a liquor that deserves respect, and keeping your ingredient list short is the best way to show it.

WAKEUP MARTINI

When you wake up in the morning, your first thought might not be of booze. But on a lazy Saturday morning, why shouldn't it be? The Wakeup Martini is the perfect breakfast cocktail, separating itself from traditional morning drinks like the Bloody Mary or Irish Coffee by adding an extra splash of breakfast flavors like maple and orange.

BASIC INGREDIENTS

 2 parts gin

 1 part triple sec

 1 splash lemon juice

 1 splash maple syrup

 1 lemon twist (garnish)

GLASSWARE:
Cocktail glass.

1. Pour the liquid ingredients into a cocktail shaker with ice and shake well to completely integrate the maple syrup.

2. Strain the resulting mixture into a Cocktail glass. Garnish with a lemon twist and enjoy!

CLASSIC GIN AND TONIC

1 part Tanqueray gin

1 part tonic water

1 splash lime juice

1 lime wedge (garnish)

Turn the page for the recipe!

→

CLASSIC GIN AND TONIC

Always start simple. The Gin and Tonic is a classic cocktail that you can order in any bar or make for yourself at home in a snap. "But," you're probably thinking, "isn't a Gin and Tonic just gin and tonic?" Alright, you've got me there. But the best part about starting with such a simple cocktail is that it has the sort of nice, clean look that classes up any occasion.

BASIC INGREDIENTS

 I part Tanqueray gin

 I part tonic water

 I splash lime juice

 I lime wedge (garnish)

 GLASSWARE:
Old Fashioned glass.

1. Fill a glass with ice and pour in the gin and tonic water. Stir until thoroughly mixed.

2. Top with a splash of lime juice. Garnish with a lime wedge and enjoy!

PERFECT GIN AND TONIC

Believe it or not, you actually can improve on the classic gin and tonic. Start by using some top-shelf gin. This recipe calls for Bombay Sapphire, but you can certainly substitute a gin such as Hendrick's if it suits you better. Also, try to tease an extra bit of flavor out of the fresh ingredients by muddling the lime juice with some fresh lime in your glass. You won't be disappointed with the results.

BASIC INGREDIENTS

 I splash lime juice

 I lime wheel (muddled)

 I part Bombay Sapphire gin

 I part tonic water

 I lime wheel (garnish)

 GLASSWARE:
Old Fashioned glass.

1. Muddle a lime wheel with fresh lime juice at the bottom of your glass. Add ice.

2. Pour in the gin and top with tonic water. Stir until thoroughly mixed.

3. Garnish with another lime wheel and enjoy!

BUDGET GIN AND TONIC

There's nothing wrong with cheaper gins like Gordon's or Seagram's. In fact, lower-shelf gin tends to be better than the lower-shelf options for most other liquors. So while you might balk at the Budget Gin and Tonic, there's really no reason to do so. It might be a bit harsher than the smooth, velvety tastes achieved by more expensive gins, but it lacks none of the flavor.

BASIC INGREDIENTS

 1 part Seagram's gin

 1 part tonic water

 1 splash lime juice

 1 lime wedge (garnish)

 GLASSWARE:
Old Fashioned glass.

1. Fill a glass with ice and pour in the gin and tonic water. Stir until thoroughly mixed. Top with a splash of lime juice.

2. Garnish with a lime wedge and enjoy!

1505 G&T

Maybe though, just maybe, what makes the Gin and Tonic special to you is the fact that it's just so drinkable. Maybe what makes the Gin and Tonic your go-to drink is the fact that you can make one as big as you want and sip on it for the next hour or two, confident that the first sip will be just as delicious as the last. Well then, the 1505 G&T is for you. Named for the address of its Connecticut waterfront birthplace, it'll keep a drink in your hand for the next hour or more, and it's the perfect way to start or end the night.

BASIC INGREDIENTS

2 parts Tanqueray gin

1 part lime juice (fresh)

4 parts tonic water

GLASSWARE:
24 oz tumbler.

1. Fill your tumbler about ¼ of the way with gin, then add ice.

2. Add the lime juice, then top off with tonic water.

3. Stir until thoroughly mixed and enjoy!

NOT-QUITE COLLINS

One of the most popular (and tasty) gin drinks is the Tom Collins, but the drink is a bit more complex than our set of rules allows. No matter—it's an easy drink to adapt in a variety of different ways! Dropping the usual dose of lime juice from the equation leaves us with something that isn't quite a Tom Collins... but is just as tasty.

BASIC INGREDIENTS

1 part gin

1 tsp sugar

1 splash lemon juice

2 parts club soda

1 orange slice (garnish)

1 maraschino cherry (garnish)

GLASSWARE:
Collins glass or Highball glass.

1. Add the gin, sugar, and lemon juice to a cocktail shaker filled with ice and shake until thoroughly mixed.

2. Strain the resulting mixture into a Collins or Highball glass. Top with club soda.

3. Garnish with an orange slice and a maraschino cherry and enjoy!

VARIATION. Since a Tom Collins usually contains both lemon juice and lime juice, feel free to swap out which one you'd prefer to use here. Only have lime juice? No worries. The flavors are slightly different but equally tasty.

ORANGE MARTINI

Martinis are delicious, but maybe a bit too simple? Add a bit of extra flavor with the Orange Martini, a delicious mixture of standard Martini flavor and citrus bite. A little bit of blood orange liqueur goes a long way here, both in terms of imparting a surprising amount of flavor and adding a flash of brightness to a typically colorless cocktail.

BASIC INGREDIENTS

 3 parts gin

 1 part dry vermouth

 1 part blood orange liqueur

 1 dash orange bitters

 1 orange twist (garnish)

GLASSWARE:
Cocktail glass.

1. Add the gin, vermouth, liqueur, and bitters to a mixing glass filled with ice and stir until thoroughly mixed.

2. Strain the resulting mixture into a Cocktail glass. Garnish with an orange twist and enjoy!

VARIATIONS. Of course, you could make a similar cocktail with any flavor you prefer. Orange is one of the best because of the unique coloration of the blood orange liqueur, but you could concoct a similar drink using cherry liqueur, watermelon liqueur, or any other flavor you've taken a shine to.

NEGRONI

Speaking of drinks with a gorgeous coloration, you probably won't find a better looking cocktail than the Negroni. Sporting a deep red hue courtesy of the sweet vermouth and Campari it prominently features, the Negroni is a delicious, gin-based answer to the famous Manhattan whiskey cocktail. Want to add a little twist on this classic cocktail? Try finishing with a dash of bitters.

BASIC INGREDIENTS

 I part gin

 I part Campari

 I part sweet vermouth

 I dash bitters

 I orange slice (garnish)

GLASSWARE:
Old Fashioned glass.

1. Add the liquid ingredients to a glass filled with ice and stir until thoroughly mixed.

2. Strain the resulting mixture into an Old Fashioned glass over ice. Garnish with an orange slice and enjoy!

GIN ROSE

Similar to the Roses for Alex drink, the Gin Rose is a brightly colored drink that maintains the perfect level of light airiness. With a slight orange twist against the boldness of the gin, the Gin Rose is a sweet little cocktail with a gorgeous red color.

BASIC INGREDIENTS

 1 part gin

 1 part triple sec

 2 parts club soda

 1 splash grenadine

 1 maraschino cherry (garnish)

GLASSWARE:
Old Fashioned glass.

1. Pour the gin and triple sec into an Old Fashioned glass over ice. Add club soda to fill and stir until thoroughly mixed.

2. Top with a splash of grenadine. Garnish with a maraschino cherry and enjoy!

SALTY MUTT

Similar to the popular Salty Dog drink, the Salty Mutt adds another flavor to the equation by splitting the usual grapefruit juice with cranberry juice. There's sticking with what works and then there's branching out into a whole new set of flavors. The Salty Dog may be an old thoroughbred, but the Salty Mutt is a boozy companion you can count on.

BASIC INGREDIENTS

 Salt (for rimming)

 I part gin

 I part grapefruit juice

 I part cranberry juice

 I grapefruit wedge (garnish)

GLASSWARE:
Old Fashioned glass.

1. Rim the glass with salt.

2. Add the gin, grapefruit juice, and cranberry juice to a cocktail shaker filled with ice. Shake vigorously.

3. Strain the resulting mixture over ice into an Old Fashioned glass—or Highball glass if you're extra thirsty.

4. Garnish with a grapefruit wedge and enjoy!

SINGAPORE EXPRESS

The Singapore Sling is an astoundingly tasty cocktail, but man is it complicated. By toning down the complexity of the flavors just a little bit, you can still mix up a fantastic cocktail that captures the essence of the Singapore Sling without taking all day to make. You don't have to graduate from mixology class to make a delicious Singapore Express. All you need is a handful of ingredients and a set of taste buds.

BASIC INGREDIENTS

 2 parts gin

 I part cherry liqueur

 I part triple sec

 3 parts pineapple juice

 I maraschino cherry (garnish)

 I slice of orange (garnish)

GLASSWARE:
Hurricane glass.

1. Pour the gin, liqueur, triple sec, and pineapple juice into a cocktail shaker filled with ice and shake vigorously.

2. Strain the resulting mixture into a Hurricane glass over ice.

3. Garnish with a maraschino cherry and a slice of orange and enjoy!

HINT OF MINT

This fizzy, ginger ale and lemonade concoction is the perfect punch for any large gathering. Just fill a punch bowl with ice and let guests go to town on this refreshing alternative to boring old fruit punches. This addition of a few mint leaves will add a subtle hint of flavor that will make partygoers say "mmm, what is that?" Makes 4 servings.

BASIC INGREDIENTS

 20 mint leaves

 1 part ginger ale

 2 parts lemonade

 1 part gin

 4 lemon wheels (garnish)

 GLASSWARE: Highball or pint glasses.

1. Tear the mint leaves in half and add them to the bottom of a pitcher. Add ice.

2. Pour in the ginger ale, lemonade, and gin, and stir until mixed.

3. Serve in individual glasses, garnish with lemon wheels and enjoy!

GIN AND JUICE

Sporting a trio of delicious fruit flavors along with the usual juniper of the gin, Gin and Juice is a delicious alternative to a simple gin and cranberry combination. The addition of a splash of triple sec and lime juice gives the drink something of a fruit salad feel and makes for a delicious and fresh-tasting drink perfect for any time of year.

BASIC INGREDIENTS

1 part gin

1 part cranberry juice

1 splash triple sec

1/2 lime (juiced)

1 lime wheel (garnish)

GLASSWARE:
Old Fashioned glass.

1. Add the gin, cranberry juice, triple sec, and lime juice to a cocktail shaker filled with ice and shake vigorously.

2. Strain the resulting mixture into a an Old Fashioned glass containing your desired amount of ice.

3. Garnish with a lime wheel and enjoy!

CHERRY GIN SOUR

There are a lot of great sour cocktails out there, but few of them contain gin. This is a shame, because, while you might not think of juniper as the perfect taste to complement a sour cocktail, gin shows a resiliency and ability to rise to the challenge of any flavor you pit against it. The Cherry Gin Sour is excellent proof of this concept, as the flavor of the gin perfectly accents the cherry and lemon.

BASIC INGREDIENTS

 I part gin

 I part cherry liqueur

 I part lemon juice

 I splash simple syrup

 I maraschino cherry (garnish)

 I orange slice (garnish)

 GLASSWARE:
Old Fashioned glass.

1. Add the gin, cherry liqueur, lemon juice, and simple syrup to a cocktail shaker filled with ice and shake well.

2. Strain the resulting mixture into an Old Fashioned glass filled with ice.

3. Garnish with a maraschino cherry and an orange slice and enjoy!

CLASSIC GIMLET

4 oz Tanqueray gin

1/2 lime (juiced)

1 lime wheel (garnish)

Turn the page for the recipe!
→

CLASSIC GIMLET

The Gimlet is as classic as it gets. Featuring just two ingredients (gin and lime), the Gimlet is gin's sour answer to the Martini. Easy to make and even easier to drink, the Classic Gimlet features half a lime's worth of juice balancing its flavor with four ounces of gin. Garnished with a lime wheel, the Classic Gimlet features fresh flavors that will never go out of style.

BASIC INGREDIENTS

4 oz Tanqueray gin

1/2 lime (juiced)

1 lime wheel (garnish)

GLASSWARE:
Cocktail glass.

1. Add the gin to a cocktail shaker filled with ice along with the juice from ½ lime. Shake until thoroughly mixed.

2. Strain the resulting mixture into a Cocktail glass.

3. Garnish with a lime wheel and enjoy!

TWISTED GIMLET

The traditional Gimlet is a classic combination of flavors, but the Twisted Gimlet asks the question "what if we could do better?" Whether the Twisted Gimlet surpasses its original inspiration is up to you, but it certainly offers something a bit different. The addition of orange bitters in particular differentiates it from the original Gimlet in a unique and delicious way.

BASIC INGREDIENTS

 2 parts gin

 1 part triple sec

 1 part lime juice

 2 drops orange bitters

 1 lime wheel (garnish)

 GLASSWARE:
Cocktail glass.

1. Add the liquid ingredients to a mixing glass filled with ice. Stir until thoroughly mixed.

2. Strain the resulting mixture into a Cocktail glass.

3. Garnish with a lime wheel and enjoy!

GIN WATERFALL

Speaking of champagne, Why not a large-batch drink that takes advantage of champagne's bubbly goodness? A little champagne and a little Sprite can complement gin quite well, creating a party punch perfect for any get together. Of course, the best part of a party punch is that you can control the strength—dial it back if you're concerned about your guests getting too drunk, or kick it up a notch if you're gearing up for a long night! *Makes 10 servings.*

BASIC INGREDIENTS

I part gin

I part champagne

2 parts Sprite

5 lemons (juiced)

20 lemon wheels (garnish, punch bowl)

GLASSWARE:
Highball glass.

1. Add all the liquid ingredients together in a large punch bowl. Make sure you have enough ice!

2. Stir together until thoroughly mixed, then add several lemons' worth of lemon wheels as a garnish. Enjoy!

MAKING A LARGE-BATCH DRINK?
Fruit slices—especially fruit wheels—are a great way to add a little extra character to your presentation. Bisect a few oranges, limes, lemons, or other fruits into circles and add them to your pitcher or punch bowl for a great look that's sure to impress.

GIN POM POM

6 mint leaves

1 part gin

1 part pomegranate juice

1 lime wedge (juiced)

1 lime wheel (garnish)

Turn the page for the recipe!
→

GIN POM POM

Pomegranate is an extremely underrated cocktail ingredient. Come to think of it, pomegranate is an extremely underrated fruit (probably because the only thing harder than retrieving the fruit from inside a pomegranate is winning a land war in Asia). So forget the fruit itself—focus on just the juice and make yourself a delicious Gin Pom Pom. With a splash of lime juice and a hint of mint, this is a drink that truly elevates its flavors.

BASIC INGREDIENTS

 6 mint leaves

 1 part gin

 1 part pomegranate juice

 1 lime wedge (juiced)

 1 lime wheel (garnish)

 GLASSWARE:
Old Fashioned glass.

1. Tear the mint leaves in half and add them to a cocktail shaker filled with ice. Add the gin, pomegranate juice, and juice from a lime wedge and shake well.

2. Strain the resulting mixture into an Old Fashioned glass filled with ice.

3. Garnish with a lime wheel and enjoy!

152

FRENCH 75

The French 75 isn't as prominent as it once was, but, if you've had one, chances are it has made its way onto your list of favorite cocktails. Gin and champagne are such a beautiful and elegant combination—the fizz of the champagne is a sweet and flavorful alternative to the club soda and tonic water that gin typically finds itself paired with. This is one drink where the garnish actually makes the drink; if you don't serve it with a lemon twist and a cherry balanced over the glass on a toothpick, you've done it wrong.

BASIC INGREDIENTS

 I sugar cube

 I lemon wedge (juiced)

 I part gin

 2 parts champagne

 I lemon twist (garnish)

 I skewered cherry (garnish)

 GLASSWARE: Champagne flute.

1. Add a sugar cube to your Champagne flute and squeeze in the juice from one lemon wedge.

2. Pour in the gin and top with champagne.

3. Garnish with a lemon wedge. Skewer a cherry with a toothpick and place it over the top of the Champagne flute. Enjoy!

MARTINI SHOOTER

This mini Martini captures all the flavors that make the Martini great while reducing it to a single gulp. Is it classy? Is it not? In this case, the answer is probably in the eye of the beholder (or the drinker). Gin generally isn't the most popular liquor to drink by the shot, but the Martini Shooter offers a delicious and, well, weirdly adorable way to develop a taste for it.

BASIC INGREDIENTS

 1 oz gin

 1/4 oz dry vermouth

 1 dash olive brine

 1 cocktail olive

 GLASSWARE:
Shot glass.

1. Mix the ingredients together in a shot glass. Add one pimento-stuffed green cocktail olive to the bottom of the glass.

2. Throw it back and enjoy! Don't forget to eat the olive—it's an essential part of the experience.

BLUEBERRY SPARKLER

2 oz gin

1 oz blueberry simple syrup

1/2 lemon (juiced)

1 oz club soda

1 lemon wheel (garnish)

Turn the page for the recipe!
→

BLUEBERRY SPARKLER

Rum isn't the only liquor that works well in an Italian soda. In fact, there's a good argument to be made that gin is the perfect liquor for that particular format. In any case, the Blueberry Sparkler takes that great gin flavor and complements it with some sweet blueberry simple syrup. A little splash of lemon juice adds some sour tartness to this drink, which is perfect for sipping on the porch on a hot summer day.

BASIC INGREDIENTS

 2 oz gin

 1 oz blueberry simple syrup

 1/2 lemon (juiced)

 1 oz club soda

 1 lemon wheel (garnish)

GLASSWARE:
 Old Fashioned glass.

1. Add the gin, blueberry simple syrup, and lemon juice to a cocktail shaker filled with ice. Shake vigorously.

2. Strain the resulting mixture into an Old Fashioned glass filled with ice. Top with club soda.

3. Garnish with a lemon wheel and enjoy!

> **WANT TO MAKE FLAVORED SIMPLE SYRUPS?** It's easier than it sounds. To infuse your simple syrup with some extra fruit flavor, just add some juice from your fruit of choice during the boiling process. Now you can add a little fruit flavor to your drinks without having to slice anything up!

SNOW BOWL

If gin evokes feelings of Christmas, the Snow Bowl should drive the point home. The flavors in this drink really work overtime to tantalize your taste buds with rich, chocolate, minty goodness. If you're looking for a rich drink that looks as good as it tastes, the Snow Bowl knocks it straight through the uprights. The slight dusting of nutmeg over this pristine white drink is as good looking as cocktails come.

 BASIC INGREDIENTS

 I part gin

 I part white chocolate liqueur

 I splash crème de menthe

 I dusting nutmeg

GLASSWARE:
Old Fashioned glass.

1. Add the gin, white chocolate liqueur, and crème de menthe to a cocktail shaker filled with ice and shake well.

2. Strain the resulting mixture into an Old Fashioned glass over ice.

3. Top with a dusting of nutmeg and enjoy!

GIN HOT CHOCOLATE

Sticking with the chocolate theme, why not add gin to a familiar winter warmer with the delicious Gin Hot Chocolate cocktail? If you like hot chocolate, there's no reason you won't love Gin Hot Chocolate as well. This boozy alternative to boring old regular hot chocolate even adds a splash of cream liqueur.

BASIC INGREDIENTS

 I part gin

 3 parts hot chocolate

 I part cream liqueur

I dollop whipped cream

GLASSWARE:

 Irish Coffee glass or mug.

1. Add gin and hot chocolate to an Irish Coffee glass.

2. Stir in cream liqueur.

3. Top with a dollop of whipped cream and enjoy!

RUBY FIZZ

The Ruby Fizz is a beautiful and delicious summer cocktail. The fizz of the club soda adds an airiness to this already light cocktail, and the bright red grenadine underscores the color of the grapefruit juice. It's a simple, elegant cocktail that anyone is sure to love.

BASIC INGREDIENTS

 I part gin

 I part grapefruit juice

 I part club soda

 I splash grenadine

 I grapefruit wedge (garnish)

 GLASSWARE: Highball glass.

1. Add your desired amount of ice to a Highball glass and pour in the gin and grapefruit juice. Stir together.

2. Add club soda to fill and stir again. Top with a splash of grenadine for color.

3. Garnish with a grapefruit wedge and enjoy!

TEQUILA

Tequila is dangerous, and that's why we love it. Whether you're drinking it in a delicious Margarita or simply sipping it on the rocks, it's hard to deny that there's something magnetic about the strangely earthy taste of tequila.

The adaptability of tequila is part of what makes it truly unique, though. Sometimes it asserts itself to the forefront of a drink's flavor profile; other times, it fades into the background, allowing other flavors to take the lead. What you get out of it depends on how you use it and how deft a hand you have when it comes to complementary flavors.

We start this chapter with margaritas, of course. But then, staying relatively basic, let's be creative and take a deep dive into the flavors that make tequila cocktails great.

CLASSIC MARGARITA

The classic to end all classics. It's not that every Margarita is perfect, but as long as the basic elements are there, chances are you're going to be just fine. The Classic Margarita uses exactly the type of tequila that most of us have lying around the house, with a splash of that traditional orange liqueur to brighten things up. Don't forget to salt the rim!

BASIC INGREDIENTS

 Salt (for rimming)

 2 parts Jose Cuervo gold tequila

 I part triple sec

 I part lime juice

 I lime slice (garnish)

 GLASSWARE:
Margarita glass.

1. Salt the rim of your Margarita glass.

2. Add the tequila, triple sec, and lime juice to a cocktail shaker filled with ice. Shake well.

3. Strain the resulting mixture into your Margarita glass over ice. Garnish with a lime slice and enjoy!

> Many cocktails can be made into a "frozen" version simply by adding a little ice and blending it all together. Frozen Margaritas are a particularly popular option. Just throw a cup or so of ice in the blender with the usual Margarita ingredients, and presto! A perfect frozen treat.

PERFECT MARGARITA

It's not a huge step up from the Classic Margarita, but it is an important one. As seasoned tequila drinkers will tell you, the difference between grabbing the first tequila you see and grabbing a bottle just one shelf higher can be huge. You don't have to break the bank though—try making a Perfect Margarita with 1800 silver tequila instead of your usual Jose Cuervo, and you'll see a huge difference. For a little extra depth of flavor, try using Grand Marnier instead of triple sec, too.

BASIC INGREDIENTS

Salt (for rimming)

2 parts 1800 silver tequila

1 part Grand Marnier

1 part lime juice

1 lime wedge (garnish)

GLASSWARE:
Margarita glass.

1. Salt the rim of your Margarita glass.

2. Add the tequila, Grand Marnier, and lime juice to a cocktail shaker filled with ice. Shake well.

3. Strain the resulting mixture into your Margarita glass over ice. Garnish with a lime wheel and enjoy!

There are dozens, hundreds, maybe even thousands of Margarita variations out there. You can use just about any flavor you like, and, as long as you include lime juice and tequila, you can probably still call it a Margarita. Some prefer sugar on the rim of their glass, but salt is traditional. Who are any of us to argue with tradition?

BUDGET MARGARITA

Bottled margarita mixes are getting tastier as companies perfect their recipes, and there's no reason to turn your nose up at the surprisingly delicious Budget Margarita.

BASIC INGREDIENTS

 Salt (for rimming)

 1 part Jose Cuervo gold tequila

 1 part Margarita mix (estimated)

 1 lime wedge (garnish)

 GLASSWARE:
Margarita glass.

1. Salt the rim of your Margarita glass.

2. Add the tequila and Margarita mix to a cocktail shaker filled with ice. Shake well.

3. Strain the resulting mixture into your Margarita glass over ice. Garnish with a lime wedge and enjoy!

Different Margarita mixes will sometimes call for different ratios. Read the bottle to check how much you should be using for optimal results. Some will even have specific tequila recommendations, but when in doubt, a mid-level gold tequila will generally work just fine.

VIRGIN MARGARITA

It's hard to replicate the delicious taste of a Margarita, but the Virgin Margarita presents something a little different. If you're able to accept that this is a different cocktail altogether, you'll almost certainly find yourself enjoying this fresh and fruity concoction. Best made with fresh lemon, lime, and orange juice, the Virgin Margarita is the perfect mocktail for morning, afternoon, or night.

BASIC INGREDIENTS

 I lime wedge (garnish)

 Salt (for rimming)

 I part lemon juice

 I part lime juice

 I part orange juice

 I part simple syrup

GLASSWARE:
Margarita glass.

1. Rub the lime along the rim of your Mason jar and rim it with salt.

2. Add the lemon juice, lime juice, orange juice, and simple syrup to a cocktail shaker filled with ice and shake until combined.

3. Add ice to your Margarita glass and strain the shaker into it. Garnish with a lime wedge and enjoy!

For a Frozen Virgin Margarita, add about a cup of ice (give or take, depending on how thick you want it to be), and blend.

SHOT OF MARG

What if you could pack all of the delicious Margarita flavor into a simple shooter? The Shot of Marg answers that question in style. With the orange and lime flavors you've come to expect from a Margarita playing off the tequila, the Shot of Marg doesn't skimp on taste. It even comes complete with a familiar salted rim!

BASIC INGREDIENTS

 Salt (for rimming)

 I oz tequila

 1/4 oz triple sec

 I lime wedge (juiced)

 GLASSWARE:
Shot glass.

1. Rim the edge of a shot glass with salt.

2. Add the tequila and triple sec to the shot glass, then squeeze in the juice from one lime wedge.

3. Lick the salt, then toss back the shot and enjoy!

COCONUT MARGARITA

You probably thought we were done with coconut rum when you left the rum section, didn't you? Well think again! Coconut rum isn't just good as the centerpiece of a drink. It's a perfect accent piece as well, and the Coconut Margarita proves it beyond a reasonable doubt. With the soft, understated flavor of coconut providing the perfect undertone beneath the tequila and lime flavor, the Coconut Margarita is sure to soon be a personal favorite of yours.

BASIC INGREDIENTS

 Coconut shavings (for rimming)

 2 parts tequila

 1 part coconut rum

 1 part lime juice

 1 lime wheel (garnish)

 GLASSWARE:
Margarita glass.

1. Rim your glass with coconut shavings (use the juice from the lime wedge to make them stick).

2. Add the tequila, coconut rum, and lime juice to a cocktail shaker filled with ice. Shake well.

3. Strain the resulting mixture into your Margarita glass. Garnish with a lime wheel and enjoy!

CHERRY LIMEADE MARGARITA

The Cherry Limeade Margarita capitalizes on the lime flavor that is an essential part of any Margarita and adds a bit of cherry flavor in place of the usual orange. The result is even more different from the standard Margarita taste than you might expect and makes for an off-kilter treat.

BASIC INGREDIENTS

 Salt (for rimming)

 2 parts tequila

 1 part cherry liqueur

 1 part lime juice

 1 lime wheel (garnish)

 GLASSWARE: Margarita glass.

1. Salt the rim of your Margarita glass.

2. Add the tequila, cherry liqueur, and lime juice to a cocktail shaker filled with ice. Shake well.

3. Strain the resulting mixture into your Margarita glass. Garnish with a lime wheel and enjoy!

TEQUILA SUNRISE

1 part tequila

1 dash lemon juice

2 parts orange juice

1 splash grenadine

1 maraschino cherry (garnish)

1 orange slice (garnish)

Turn the page for the recipe!

TEQUILA SUNRISE

The (maybe) more popular sister drink to the Vodka Sunrise, the Tequila Sunrise makes use of the same vivid coloration to present a drink that is both delicious and beautiful to behold. Combining the ever-popular flavors of tequila and orange juice, along with an accent of grenadine, the Tequila Sunrise is a drink that absolutely lives up to its billing.

BASIC INGREDIENTS

 1 part tequila

 1 dash lemon juice

 2 parts orange juice

 1 splash grenadine

 1 maraschino cherry (garnish)

 1 orange slice (garnish)

 GLASSWARE: Highball glass.

1. Add ice to a Highball glass and pour in the tequila and a dash of lemon juice. Mix together.

2. Add orange juice to fill, then top with a splash of grenadine. Don't stir the drink. Instead allow the grenadine to slowly filter down through the orange juice and tequila.

3. Garnish with a maraschino cherry and an orange slice and enjoy!

VARIATION. If this sounds enticing but you're fresh out of tequila, go back to the Vodka Sunrise (page 54).

VIRGIN SUNRISE

Drinks bearing the "sunrise" name are a rare breed in that they tend to be as delicious as they are beautiful. The Virgin Sunrise makes the argument that you don't need booze to create a perfectly acceptable (and naturally delicious) variant. The Virgin Sunrise is as easy to make as adding a splash of grenadine to your orange juice, but the subtle flavor it adds and gorgeous coloration it creates make this a mocktail worth trying.

BASIC INGREDIENTS

 I glass orange juice

 I splash grenadine

 I orange wheel (garnish)

 GLASSWARE:
Hurricane glass.

1. Add orange juice to a glass over ice.

2. Top with a splash of grenadine.

3. Garnish with an orange wheel and enjoy!

DARK WINGS

Similar to the popular El Diablo cocktail, the Dark Wings drink uses tequila and lime juice coupled with a dark liqueur to create a medley of surprisingly light flavors. The bite of the ginger beer pairs well with tequila, and the blackberry liqueur and lime help to add some sweet and sour elements to the drink.

BASIC INGREDIENTS

 I part silver tequila

 I part blackberry liqueur

 I lime (juiced)

 2 parts ginger beer

 I handful blackberries (garnish)

GLASSWARE:
Highball glass.

1. Add the tequila, blackberry liqueur, and lime juice to a cocktail shaker filled with ice. Shake well.

2. Strain the resulting mixture into a Highball glass filled with ice. Top with ginger beer.

3. Garnish with a handful of blackberries and enjoy!

VARIATION. If you don't have blackberries on hand, other garnish options include a lime wedge, a cherry, or a slice of kiwi—or all three.

PALOMA PLUS

The simple Paloma is a mix of complementary flavors: one part tequila, three parts grapefruit soda. But why stop there when there are so many other flavors that accent these so well? A splash of grapefruit juice can elevate the grapefruit soda, and a bit of fresh lime juice is a plus in just about any cocktail.

BASIC INGREDIENTS

 I part tequila

 I splash grapefruit juice

 I lime wedge (juiced)

 2 parts Fresca (grapefruit soda)

 I grapefruit wedge (garnish)

 GLASSWARE: Highball glass.

1. Add the tequila, grapefruit juice, and lime juice to a Highball glass filled with ice. Mix together.

2. Top with Fresca and stir again. Garnish with a grapefruit wedge and enjoy!

TEQUILA GRAPEFRUIT COCKTAIL

Tequila and orange are an essential part of any Margarita, but they have applications outside of that traditional cocktail as well. The Tequila Grapefruit Cocktail adds in a healthy dose of a different citrus fruit, and it is an extremely welcome addition to this fresh, fruity drink. It's a refreshing drink for any time of year and a go-to morning drink for those looking for an a.m. treat.

BASIC INGREDIENTS

 I part gold tequila

 I part ginger ale

 2 parts grapefruit juice

 I dash orange liqueur

 I grapefruit slice (garnish)

 I maraschino cherry (garnish)

GLASSWARE:
 Highball glass.

1. Add ice to a Highball glass, then add the the tequila, ginger ale, grapefruit juice, and orange liqueur.

2. Stir until thoroughly mixed.

3. Garnish with a grapefruit slice and a cherry.

VARATION. If you don't have a grapefruit slice available, an orange slice will do.

186

MEXICAN MULE

Like the Moscow Mule (or the Mint Mule, see page 29), the Mexican Mule takes advantage of the distinctive taste of lime and ginger beer to craft a memorable and delicious cocktail. Whereas the Mint Mule added a bit of mint to provide a unique spin on a classic recipe, for the Mexican Mule we'll add a splash of triple sec to create a flavor profile that begs you to remember your last Margarita.

BASIC INGREDIENTS

 1 part tequila

 1 splash triple sec

 1 lime wedge (juiced)

 2 parts ginger beer

 1 lime wheel (garnish)

 GLASSWARE:
Highball glass
(or copper mug).

1. Pour the tequila and triple sec together, then squeeze in the juice from one lime wedge.

2. Top with ginger beer and stir until thoroughly mixed.

3. Garnish with a lime wheel and enjoy!

BAJA LEMONADE

1 sprig rosemary

1 part tequila

1 splash coconut rum

2 parts lemonade

1 lemon wheel (garnish)

Turn the page for the recipe!

BAJA LEMONADE

Yes, more coconut rum! And why not, when you want to evoke tropical flavors? Baja Lemonade is more than just a simple tequila and lemonade concoction, adding a bit of coconut and rosemary to the party to ensure that the depth of flavor transcends the simplistic. Maybe a standard tequila and lemonade is more your speed, but if you're looking for something a little bit out there, Baja Lemonade is the drink for you.

BASIC INGREDIENTS

1 sprig rosemary

1 part tequila

1 splash coconut rum

2 parts lemonade

1 lemon wheel (garnish)

GLASSWARE:
Highball glass.

1. Add the rosemary, tequila, and coconut rum to a cocktail shaker filled with ice. Shake vigorously.

2. Strain the mixture into a Highball glass over ice. Top with lemonade.

3. Garnish with a lemon wheel and enjoy!

VIRGIN BAJA LEMONADE

The added coconut flavor is a big part of what makes the Baja Lemonade such a delicious treat, and there's no reason you can't capture that same delicious flavor profile without the need for any pesky tequila. Instead, simply add in a bit of agave syrup as a sweetener, and go with coconut flavoring rather than coconut rum. The result is a tasty treat for a summer's day that is a creative departure from regular old lemonade.

BASIC INGREDIENTS

 5 parts lemonade

 1 part coconut syrup

 1 splash agave syrup

 1 sprig rosemary

 1 lemon wheel (garnish)

 GLASSWARE:
Highball glass.

1. Fill a cocktail shaker with ice, the liquid ingredients, and rosemary. Shake well.

2. Strain the resulting mixture into a Highball glass over ice.

3. Garnish with a lemon wheel and enjoy!

CANCUN COFFEE

Irish Coffee. Cuban Coffee. Why not Cancun Coffee? The rounded flavor of the tequila pairs surprisingly well with coffee—a bolder man than I might even say better than the whiskey in Irish Coffee. A bit of coffee and cream liqueur complete this delicious treat. Need a boost to keep you going but don't want to sacrifice your buzz? Cancun Coffee is the way to go.

BASIC INGREDIENTS

 1 part tequila

 1 part coffee liqueur

 2 parts coffee

 1 splash cream liqueur

 GLASSWARE:
Irish Coffee glass or mug.

1. Add tequila and coffee liqueur to an Irish Coffee glass. Top with coffee.

2. Finish with a splash of cream liqueur and stir until thoroughly mixed. Enjoy!

EARLY NIGHT

The Early Night is a drink so delicious that you might forget how strong it is. In fact, it's so deceptively strong that enough of them might end your night before it even begins, hence its name. But if you can handle your alcohol and you're after flavor, you could do worse than starting your night with one or two of these.

BASIC INGREDIENTS

 I part tequila

 I part cherry liqueur

 1/2 lime (juiced)

 2 parts orange juice

 Sliced starfruit (garnish)

 I maraschino cherry (garnish)

 GLASSWARE: Highball glass.

1. Add the tequila and cherry liqueur to your Highball glass over ice. Squeeze in the juice from ½ of a lime.

2. Top with orange juice and stir until thoroughly mixed. Garnish with a slice of starfruit and a cherry and enjoy!

VARIATIONS

■ If cherry isn't your favorite flavor, feel free to mix in a different type of liqueur. Melon liqueur and limoncello work almost as well, or you can choose your own!

■ If starfruit is too fancy for you, an orange wheel does the trick.

END OF THE LIME

Tequila and lime is a combination seemingly as old as liquor itself, and the reason should be obvious. There are few flavor combinations that enjoy such consistent success in the cocktail world, and whether you're taking shots or mixing cocktails, these two ingredients are never far from each other. Try mixing some tequila into a little lemon-lime soda and add some fresh lime juice to really bring out the flavor!

BASIC INGREDIENTS

I part tequila

1/2 lime (juiced)

2 parts Sprite
(or lemon-lime soda)

I lime wedge (garnish)

GLASSWARE:
Highball glass.

1. Pour the tequila over ice and add the juice from ½ lime. Top with Sprite.

2. Garnish with a lime wedge and enjoy!

BLOODY MARIA EXPRESS

As with the Bloody Mary, the Bloody Maria Express is a traditional morning cocktail that can help you kick any hangover. Trimmed down a bit from the standard Bloody Maria, which tends to be overflowing with ingredients, the Bloody Maria Express reduces the drink to its bare essentials. After all, the real joy of any of the Bloody Mary's countless variations lies in the absurd garnishes. Be creative!

BASIC INGREDIENTS

 I dash Worcestershire sauce

 I dash lemon juice

 I part tequila

 2 parts tomato juice

 Anything your heart desires (garnish)

 GLASSWARE: Pint glass.

1. Add the Worcestershire sauce and lemon juice to a pint glass, then add ice.

2. Pour in the tequila and tomato juice and stir until thoroughly mixed.

3. Garnish with anything you want— lemon, lime, cilantro, olives, or even bacon.

BERRY BURSTER

1 Kiwi (sliced)

4 strawberries (sliced)

1 part tequila

1 part strawberry Kiwi juice

Turn the page for the recipe!

BERRY BURSTER

When it comes to fresh fruit, why stop at just the juice? Sure, lime juice, lemon juice, apple juice, and other fresh fruit juices can be extremely useful and flavorful additions to any cocktail. But sometimes, adding the fruit itself to the cocktail can take a drink to the next level. Of course, the best part of adding fresh fruit to a cocktail is that when you're done, you've got a delicious treat that's been soaking up all the boozy goodness while you drink.

BASIC INGREDIENTS

 1 Kiwi (sliced)

 4 strawberries (sliced)

 1 part tequila

 1 part strawberry Kiwi juice

 GLASSWARE:
Old Fashioned glass.

1. Peel and slice the kiwi, then hull and slice the strawberries. Save a slice of kiwi as a garnish, then muddle together the rest of the sliced fruit in the bottom of a glass.

2. Add ice to the glass, then add the tequila and strawberry kiwi juice.

3. Garnish with a slice of kiwi and enjoy! Don't forget to eat the booze-infused fruit when you finish!

> **PATIENCE IS A VIRTUE.** If you're making a drink that involves slices of fruit or other edible ingredients, you might consider sealing it up and leaving it in the fridge overnight. Not only will it ensure that you have a crisp, cool beverage the next day, but it will give the drink extra time to soak into the fruit!

APPLE TART

Why do so many tequila drinks feature sweet and sour flavors like apple and lime? Because they just work so well together. The Apple Tart features the pucker-worthy sourness of apple schnapps and lime juice, tempered with a little bit of sweet apple juice. Similar in flavor and color to the ever-popular Appletini, the Apple Tart is an off-the-beaten-path tequila drink for anytime.

BASIC INGREDIENTS

2 oz tequila

1 oz apple schnapps

1 oz apple juice

1 lime (juiced)

GLASSWARE:

Highball glass.

1. Add the ingredients to a cocktail shaker filled with ice. Shake vigorously.

2. Fill a Highball glass with ice and strain the tequila mixture into it. Enjoy!

VARIATION.

Any apple juice will do for the Apple Tart, but if you have access to fresh apple juice or can juice it yourself, you may find the added freshness well worth it.

TEQUILA SPARKLER

If you like a little carbonation with your tequila cocktails but aren't interested in going the easy route with cola or ginger ale, the Tequila Sparkler might be for you. Integrating the bubbly sweetness of champagne will leave you feeling fresh, especially after you squeeze in a little bit of that fresh lime juice familiar to so many tequila cocktail recipes. It's the perfect cocktail for a New Year's Eve party or other festive celebration!

BASIC INGREDIENTS

1 part tequila

1 splash lime juice

3 parts champagne

1 lime wedge (garnish)

GLASSWARE:
Champagne flute.

1. Pour tequila and lime juice into a Champagne flute. Top with champagne.

2. Garnish with a lime wedge and enjoy!

TEQUILA LIME SODA

Simple, like an Italian soda, and just as delicious—the Tequila Lime Soda combines two very simple and distinct flavors known to play well with one another and tops them off with a fresh, fizzy splash of club soda. Some drinks really benefit from that extra fizz, and the Tequila Lime Soda is one of them. With a light and airy feel and the same great flavor you expect from a tequila and lime concoction, this is a drink that proves that less can be more.

BASIC INGREDIENTS

 I part silver tequila

 I part lime juice

 3 parts club soda

 I lime wedge (garnish)

 GLASSWARE:
Old Fashioned glass.

1. Pour the tequila and lime into your glass over ice. Stir lightly.

2. Top with club soda.

3. Garnish with a lime wedge and enjoy!

WHISKEY

A traditional Irish folk song says, "Whiskey you're the devil." But that couldn't be more wrong. In any of its forms, whiskey is a delight. Whether it's the peaty, smokiness of a well-aged scotch, the oaky goodness of bourbon, or even the full-bodied taste of a nice rye whiskey, whiskey has something to offer a wide variety of different cocktails. And as any whiskey enthusiast will tell you, even consuming the delicious beverage on its own is a treat.

The beauty of whiskey of any kind is that it lends itself well to simple cocktails. Those who enjoy whiskey enjoy it for its taste, and so it should come as no surprise that whiskey cocktails tend to accent the taste of the whiskey rather than drown it out, a la vodka. Common ingredients are accents such as simple sugar, maraschino cherries, sweet vermouth, and other more subtle flavors that don't run the risk of overwhelming the flavor of the whiskey itself.

Whiskey cocktails tend to best serve the whiskey lover. If you don't consider yourself a fan of the dark liquor, chances are these cocktails aren't for you. But if you're a whiskey enthusiast, you may find yourself unable to stop drinking these delicious concoctions. Come to think of it, maybe the song is right.

CLASSIC OLD FASHIONED

It's hard to anoint a "favorite" whiskey cocktail, but the Old Fashioned certainly challenges for the spot. Featuring just sugar, bitters, and a little bit of citrus to accent the flavor of the whiskey, the Old Fashioned is a sophisticated drink for the seasoned whiskey drinker. For the Classic version of the cocktail, an underrated, extremely drinkable whiskey like Maker's Mark will serve your purposes perfectly.

BASIC INGREDIENTS

 1 splash simple syrup

 1 strip orange rind

 2 drops bitters

 2 oz Maker's Mark Bourbon Whiskey

 1 maraschino cherry (garnish)

 GLASSWARE:
Old Fashioned Glass.

1. Add the simple syrup to an Old Fashioned glass and drop in a slice of orange rind. Add the bitters and muddle together.

2. Fill the glass with ice, then add your bourbon. Stir together slowly.

3. Garnish with a maraschino cherry and enjoy!

VARIATION. Some versions of the Old Fashioned call for the inclusion of club soda to give the drink a bit of fizz. This isn't traditionally included, but as always, it's up to you what you think you might enjoy best.

PERFECT
OLD FASHIONED

For the Perfect Old Fashioned, eschew the simple syrup in favor of a sugar cube and some water, and rely on the garnishes for the small punch of citrus that the drink requires. Using a top-shelf whiskey like Woodford Reserve will enhance the drinkability of the cocktail, while still keeping you in a reasonably accessible price range. Sure, you could spend hundreds of dollars on bourbon. But if you do that, you probably aren't watering it down with a cocktail, no matter how delicious it may be.

BASIC INGREDIENTS

 I sugar cube

 2 drops bitters

 I splash water

 2 oz Woodford Reserve Bourbon Whiskey

 I orange slice (garnish)

I maraschino cherry (garnish)

 GLASSWARE:
Old Fashioned Glass.

1. Add the sugar cube to your glass. Saturate with bitters. Add a small splash of water and muddle.

2. Fill the glass with ice and add the bourbon. Stir lightly. Garnish with a slice of orange and a maraschino cherry and enjoy!

BUDGET OLD FASHIONED

On the other hand, why go all out when there are plenty of perfectly affordable whiskeys that will do just fine? Take Evan Williams Bourbon Whiskey, for example. A decent-tasting, budget-friendly alternative to expensive options like Woodford Reserve or even Maker's Mark. When you're craving a cocktail, you're not necessarily craving the best, most expensive ingredients. You're craving a way to scratch that itch, and the Budget Old Fashioned will do the job just fine.

BASIC INGREDIENTS

 1 splash simple syrup

 2 drops bitters

 1 maraschino cherry

 2 oz Evan Williams Bourbon Whiskey

 GLASSWARE:
Old Fashioned glass.

1. Add the simple syrup, bitters, and maraschino cherry to your glass. Muddle together.

2. Fill the glass with ice. Add bourbon and stir lightly. Enjoy!

WHISKEY SOUR

Ah yes, the famous Whiskey Sour. Made a variety of different ways, sometimes with egg whites, sometimes with sour mix, and sometimes simply made with lemon juice. The drink is as sour as its name implies, adding an unexpected new dimension to the whiskey. The Whiskey Sour takes whiskey and lemon juice and smashes them together head on, creating this delicious, classic concoction.

BASIC INGREDIENTS

 2 1/2 oz rye whiskey

 1 oz lemon juice

 1/3 oz simple syrup

 1 maraschino cherry (garnish)

 1 orange slice (garnish)

 GLASSWARE:
Sour glass.

1. Add the whiskey, lemon juice, and simple syrup to a Cocktail glass filled with ice. Shake vigorously.

2. Strain the resulting mixture into a Sour glass over ice.

3. Garnish with a maraschino cherry and a slice of orange and enjoy!

BUDGET SOUR

One of the great things about living in the modern age is the convenience. There are microwave dinners, there is juice in a pouch, and anyone who doesn't feel like mixing a cocktail can go out and buy a mix to make their lives easier. As far as mixes go, sour mix is probably one of the more popular options and makes the Budget Sour a convenient, hassle-free alternative to the traditional Whiskey Sour.

BASIC INGREDIENTS

 1 part rye whiskey

 2 parts sour mix

 1 lemon slice

 GLASSWARE:
Sour glass.

1. Add the whiskey and sour mix to a Sour glass over ice. Stir until thoroughly mixed.

2. Garnish with a lemon slice and enjoy!

Different mixes from different companies may recommend mixing in different proportions. Be sure to read the label on the packaging to know for sure, but 2:1 is usually a good mix.

CLASSIC MANHATTAN

2 oz Knob Creek Rye Whiskey

2/3 oz sweet vermouth

2 drops bitters

Cherries (garnish)

Turn the page for the recipe!

→

CLASSIC MANHATTAN

Whiskey and vermouth is a classic combination, and one with which it's difficult to go wrong. The Manhattan makes use of this simple combination and, with the addition of just a few drops of bitters, creates something truly fantastic. A refined and elegant cocktail, the Classic Manhattan offers the everyday mixologist a simple way to enjoy an old classic.

BASIC INGREDIENTS

 2 oz Knob Creek Rye Whiskey

 2/3 oz sweet vermouth

 2 drops bitters

 Cherries (garnish)

GLASSWARE:
Cocktail glass.

1. Fill a mixing glass with ice and add the liquid ingredients together. Stir gently to avoid clouding the drink.

2. Strain the resulting mixture into a Cocktail glass.

3. Garnish with a cherry or two and enjoy!

If you've ever heard someone talk about not wanting to "bruise" their drink, you might have wondered what they meant. A bruised drink is a drink that contains more water than it should, which can leave it with a muddier appearance. Usually this is in reference to whiskey, but also sometimes gin. Bruising usually occurs when a cocktail is shaken.

PERFECT MANHATTAN

When it comes to a cocktail as classy as the Manhattan, why settle for anything less than the finest ingredients? By building your drink around top-shelf whiskey, you can be sure that you're getting the best tasting Manhattan around. The Perfect Manhattan is made using Whistlepig Straight Rye Whiskey, one of the most delicious whiskeys the average person can get their hands on.

BASIC INGREDIENTS

 2 oz Whistlepig Straight Rye Whiskey

 2/3 oz sweet vermouth

 2 drops bitters

 1 maraschino cherry (garnish)

 GLASSWARE: Cocktail glass.

1. Fill a mixing glass with ice and add the liquid ingredients together. Stir gently to avoid clouding the drink.

2. Put a maraschino cherry in the bottom of an Old Fashioned glass and strain the liquid ingredients over it. Enjoy!

BUDGET MANHATTAN

One of the great things about the Manhattan is its adaptability. While tradition dictates that it be made with rye whiskey, contemporary mixologists have begun to use bourbon with increasing regularity. And chances are, you're more likely to have some affordable bourbon lying around than you are rye whiskey. So why not make a Budget Manhattan? It might not be by the book (although if you're following these instructions, it technically is now), but it still packs a punch, as well as a rich, delicious flavor.

BASIC INGREDIENTS

 2 oz Jim Beam Bourbon

 2/3 oz sweet vermouth

 2 drops bitters

 1 maraschino cherry (garnish)

 GLASSWARE:
Old Fashioned glass.

1. Fill a mixing glass with ice and add the bourbon, vermouth, and bitters together. Stir gently to avoid clouding the drink.

2. Strain the mixture into an Old Fashioned or Cocktail glass. Garnish with a cherry.

ROB ROY

2 oz Scotch whiskey

1 oz sweet vermouth

2 drops bitters

1 maraschino cherry (garnish)

Turn the page for the recipe!
→

ROB ROY

The Rob Roy is, essentially, a Manhattan for those who prefer Scotch. Again made with simply whiskey, vermouth, and bitters, the Rob Roy swaps out rye whiskey (or bourbon) in favor of the smoky flavor of Scotch. The Rob Roy hasn't gained quite the same level of popularity as its rye-based contemporary, but it is no less delicious for it. As with many cocktails, your stance on the matter likely comes down to personal preference.

BASIC INGREDIENTS

 2 oz Scotch whiskey

 I oz sweet vermouth

 2 drops bitters

 I maraschino cherry (garnish)

 GLASSWARE: Cocktail glass.

1. Fill a mixing glass with ice and add the liquid ingredients together. Stir gently to avoid clouding the drink.

2. Add a maraschino cherry to your Cocktail glass and strain the resulting mixture over it. Enjoy!

CLASSIC MINT JULEP

Who doesn't love a Mint Julep? The classic drink of the Kentucky Derby, the Mint Julep has remained popular with whiskey drinkers for over 100 years. With a mid-range, drinkable bourbon and a little powdered sugar (the powdered sugar is important if you want to do it right), this is a cocktail sure to see many new converts after just one taste.

BASIC INGREDIENTS

 4 mint leaves

 1 tsp powdered sugar

 1 splash water

 2 oz Maker's Mark Bourbon Whiskey

 1 mint sprig (garnish)

 GLASSWARE:
Old Fashioned glass.

1. Tear the mint leaves in half to release their flavor, then muddle in the bottom of your glass with powdered sugar and water.

2. Fill the glass with cracked ice, then add the bourbon. Stir gently.

3. Garnish with a sprig of mint and enjoy!

PERFECT MINT JULEP

Why not take the Mint Julep to a bit more of a high-end place? If you truly appreciate subtle flavor and nuance (and are willing to spend a bit extra on the best bourbon), you can make your Mint Julep into a truly transcendent drinking experience. Be sure you drink it out of a silver or pewter cup—if you're going to call something "perfect," you'd better go all the way. The Perfect Mint Julep does just that.

BASIC INGREDIENTS

 4 mint leaves

 1 tsp powdered sugar

 1 splash water

 2 oz Woodford Reserve Bourbon Whiskey

 1 mint sprig (garnish)

 GLASSWARE:
Silver or pewter cup.

1. Muddle the mint leaves in the bottom of the cup with powdered sugar and water.

2. Fill the cup with cracked ice, then add your bourbon. Stir until the outside of your cup is visibly chilled.

3. Garnish with a sprig of mint and enjoy!

BUDGET MINT JULEP

So you want a Mint Julep, but you don't have the ingredients to do it exactly as described. No matter. There are plenty of ways to make a perfectly acceptable Mint Julep with whatever you happen to have on hand. The beauty of the Mint Julep is that while it has a reputation for being a refined cocktail, the ingredients are simple enough that just about anyone should be able to make it (as long as you've got some mint on hand!).

BASIC INGREDIENTS

 4 mint leaves

 1 tsp sugar

 1 splash water

 2 oz Evan Williams Bourbon Whiskey

 1 mint sprig (garnish)

 GLASSWARE:
Highball glass.

1. Never mind the powdered sugar; regular sugar will work just fine. Muddle the sugar in your glass with the water and mint leaves (tear them in half to release additional flavor).

2. Fill the glass with ice, then add your bourbon.

3. Garnish with a sprig of mint and enjoy!

WHALEN SMASH

Whiskey and ginger is a time-honored flavor combination, but precious few whiskey cocktails do an adequate job including mint. The Whalen Smash forgoes the ginger liqueurs that similar cocktails often call for, instead adding a splash of ginger ale to give the drink some added lightness. The carbonation gives the drink a playful element, but doesn't overwhelm the palate, leaving plenty of room for the mint and lemon to play off one another.

BASIC INGREDIENTS

 1/2 lemon, cut into thirds

 4 mint leaves

 3 parts bourbon whiskey

 1 part ginger beer

GLASSWARE:
 Old Fashioned glass.

1. Squeeze the lemon wedges into your glass. Drop the squeezed wedges into the glass.

2. Add the mint to the glass and muddle with the lemon juice. Add ice as desired.

3. Pour in the bourbon, then top with a splash of ginger beer. Stir together and enjoy!

VARIATION. A slice of lime is always welcome.

CINNAMON APPLE

2 parts apple cider

1 part apple liqueur

1 part cinnamon whiskey

1 cinnamon stick (garnish)

Turn the page for the recipe!

→

CINNAMON APPLE

Whether in an apple pie or an apple crumble, there are few flavors that go together more perfectly than cinnamon and apple. It might even be called the quintessential flavor of our land—after all, what's more American than apple pie? But pies are work, and they take time. Why spend the whole day preparing an apple pie when you can *drink* one instead? The Cinnamon Apple cocktail features the delicious flavors you expect from your favorite homemade treats, but with a delightful buzz in lieu of the sugar rush.

BASIC INGREDIENTS

 2 parts apple cider

 1 part apple liqueur

 1 part cinnamon whiskey

 1 cinnamon stick (garnish)

GLASSWARE:
 Old Fashioned glass.

1. Fill an Old Fashioned glass with ice and add the cider, apple liqueur, and cinnamon whiskey. Stir until thoroughly mixed.

2. Garnish with a cinnamon stick and enjoy!

VARIATIONS

- To soften the flavor a bit, add a bit of Amaretto or even some Orgeat syrup.
- If the tartness of the apple liqueur is overwhelming, you can also omit it in favor of just cider and whiskey.

VIRGIN
CINNAMON APPLE

Cinnamon and apple are a celebrated flavor combination that extends well beyond alcoholic beverages. Here, sparkling cider, cinnamon, and a cinnamon stick transform apple cider into a delicious fall mocktail.

BASIC INGREDIENTS

 2 parts apple cider

1 part sparkling cider

 1 dash cinnamon

 1 cinnamon stick (garnish)

GLASSWARE:
Old Fashioned glass
(or wine goblet).

1. Fill a glass with ice and add the ciders and cinnamon. Stir until mixed.

2. Garnish with a cinnamon stick and enjoy!

MISH MASH

Ever forget to restock your liquor cabinet for a few weeks, or maybe even months? Once in a while, you open the cabinet and realize you're left with just a handful of odds and ends that don't really make anything. The Mish Mash takes a couple of odds and ends that you should always have a half bottle of or so, mixes in a bit of bourbon, and gives you a surprisingly delicious result.

BASIC INGREDIENTS

2 parts bourbon whiskey

1 part triple sec

1 part simple syrup

1 splash grenadine

GLASSWARE:
Old Fashioned glass.

1. Fill a glass with ice and add bourbon, triple sec, and simple syrup.

2. Stir together until mixed. Top with a splash of grenadine and enjoy!

VARIATION. Feel free to swap out the triple sec for a different type of liqueur, such as raspberry, strawberry, or lemon.

IRISH ROSE

With its rosy coloration and whiskey-heavy flavor, the Irish Rose is a tasty alternative to the more common whiskey cocktails. The unusual combination of whiskey and Sprite works surprisingly well, especially with the thickness and subtle flavor of grenadine helping to bridge the gap between the two distinct flavor profiles.

BASIC INGREDIENTS

2 parts Irish whiskey

3 parts Sprite

1 part grenadine

1 lemon wedge (garnish)

GLASSWARE:
Old Fashioned glass.

1. Add ice to your glass, then add in the whiskey and Sprite.

2. Top with a splash of grenadine and stir together until a rosy color is achieved.

3. Garnish with a wedge of lemon and enjoy!

The great thing about most cocktails is that they're so easy to tweak to fit your purposes. If you have a favorite cocktail but don't have all of the ingredients, it can be a rewarding experience to play around and see if you can use what you have to create something just as tasty!

IRISH COFFEE

The perfect wake-up cocktail and a favorite drink of airport bar patrons (or maybe that's just me). Irish Coffee is made a variety of different ways, with some including Irish Cream, some not, some specifying Irish whiskey, some not. But it just doesn't feel like "Irish" Coffee without Jameson and Bailey's, does it?

BASIC INGREDIENTS

 3 parts coffee

 1 dash sugar

 1 part Jameson Irish Whiskey

 1 part Bailey's Irish Cream

 Whipped cream (garnish)

 GLASSWARE:
Irish Coffee glass or mug.

1. Pour the coffee into your glass or mug and add sugar. Stir until the sugar has dissolved.

2. Add whiskey and stir again.

3. Top with Irish cream. If you can, layer the cream on top rather than stirring it in.

4. If desired, garnish with a dollop of whipped cream on top and enjoy!

BOURBON SWEET TEA

Bourbon is a favorite drink of the south, and so is sweet tea. What could be more natural than adding them together to create a refreshing and delicious beverage perfect for beating the heat? It's the perfect spur-of-the-moment drink, devoid of fancy ingredients or complicated instructions. Just mix your tea and bourbon with a little bit of lemon and enjoy! *Makes 4 servings.*

BASIC INGREDIENTS

 1/2 lemon (juiced)

 1 part bourbon

 4 parts sweet tea

 4 lemon wheels (garnish)

 GLASSWARE:
Pint glass.

1. Squeeze the juice from ½ lemon into a pitcher. Add the juiced portion to the pitcher.

2. Add ice, then pour in the bourbon and sweet tea. Stir until thoroughly mixed.

3. Pour into individual glasses and garnish each with a lemon wheel. Enjoy!

VARIATION. Sweet tea too overwhelming for you? You can always make this drink with unsweetened fresh-brewed iced tea.

Store-bought iced teas and lemonades work just fine, but if you're feeling particularly industrious you might want to make your own. Play around with the proportion of lemon and sugar until you find a lemonade mixture you're happy with, or throw a bunch of your favorite tea bags into some boiling water and let it brew for a while. It might be harder than just pouring it out of a bottle, but you'll be surprised at how much better it will taste!

A LITTLE OF THIS, A LITTLE OF THAT

What about drinks that don't fall into any particular category? You know the ones. Made with champagne, made with beer, made with vermouth or even brandy or wine. These drinks deserve our love, too.

After all, where would we be without a nice Mimosa or glass of Sangria on a Saturday morning? And how are you supposed to impress your friends with your knowledge of unusual (yet elegant) cocktails without an Americano recipe?

These miscellaneous cocktails may not fit into any of the major liquor categories, but they are no less delicious for it. Chances are you'll find something that makes you wonder why you never thought of it yourself.

MIMOSA

The perfect drink for Saturday morning! How could you not love Mimosas? Sure, some people might not like Bloody Marys. If you don't like tomato juice, they might not be your thing. And if you're not a coffee drinker, the Irish Coffee is out. But with a simple mixture of citrusy orange juice and bubbly champagne, the Mimosa stands apart as a fantastic cocktail offering something for everyone.

BASIC INGREDIENTS

 1 part orange juice

 1 part champagne

 1 orange slice (garnish)

 GLASSWARE:
Champagne flute.

1. Fill your Champagne flute halfway with orange juice.

2. Top off with champagne. Stir if you want, or let them combine on their own. Garnish with a slice of orange and enjoy!

VIRGIN MIMOSA

Mimosas are great, but sometimes you just aren't ready to start drinking that early. Perfectly understandable. Still, the bubbly lightness of a Mimosa offers something far beyond just a simple buzz. You're in luck! In place of champagne, you can opt for a simple splash of Sprite in your drink, giving the orange juice a little extra kick and starting your day right!

BASIC INGREDIENTS

 I part orange juice

 I part Sprite

 I orange slice (garnish)

GLASSWARE:
Champagne flute.

1. Fill your Champagne flute halfway with orange juice.

2. Top off with Sprite and stir together.

3. Garnish with a slice of orange and enjoy!

VARIATION. Sprite not your thing? Try it with ginger ale instead!

Champagne is an easy ingredient to substitute out when it comes to making virgin drinks. Its chief attribute is its fizzy sweetness, and a simple switch to Sprite, ginger ale, or even sparkling cider can turn a tasty cocktail into an equally delicious mocktail!

SANGRIA EXPRESS

1 orange (1/2 juiced, 1/2 peeled and thinly sliced)

6 oz brandy

1 bottle red wine

4 oz simple syrup

Turn the page for the recipe!
→

SANGRIA EXPRESS

The beauty of Sangria tends to be the inclusion of as many different fruits as possible, but most of us don't have the luxury of an entire fruit market at our fingertips every day. So forget Sangria—go the express route and mix in a few complementary flavors for a morning beverage that's just as delicious! Makes 4-6 servings.

BASIC INGREDIENTS

 1 orange (1/2 juiced, 1/2 peeled and thinly sliced)

 6 oz brandy

1 bottle red wine

 4 oz simple syrup

 GLASSWARE:
Wine glass.

1. Juice half of the orange into a sealable container. Peel and slice the other half, and put those slices into the same container.

2. Add the brandy, red wine, and simple syrup.

3. Seal the container and refrigerate for 24 hours.

4. Pour into a pitcher or punch bowl and enjoy!

DON'T FEEL LIKE WAITING? You can always skip it. The flavors won't combine quite as well (and the fruit won't soak up the flavor quite so much), but it will still be delicious! Feel free to use a fruit other than orange, too.

VIRGIN SANGRIA EXPRESS

At its core, Sangria is fruit juice. Much of that fruit happens to be wine, but that's okay. Virgin Sangria takes that same great, grape-based flavor, and builds around it. Adding apple, orange, and lemon juice (along with some slices of fresh orange to soak up flavor), the Virgin Sangria Express is a great alternative to its more boozy counterpart. Makes 4-6 servings.

BASIC INGREDIENTS

 4 oranges (3 juiced, 1 peeled and thinly sliced)

 12 oz grape juice

 6 oz apple juice

 2 oz lemon juice

 GLASSWARE: Wine glass.

1. Juice three oranges into a large, sealable container. Peel and slice the other orange, and put those slices into the same container.

2. Add the grape juice, apple juice, and lemon juice.

3. Seal the container and refrigerate for 24 hours.

4. Pour into a pitcher or punch bowl and enjoy!

Always feel free to add in any fresh fruit you desire. Nothing tastes quite as great as fruit that's been soaking up the delicious flavors of Sangria, virgin or otherwise!

AMERICANO

You might not know it, thanks to the later popularity of the Vodka Martini, but the Americano was actually the original drink of that most famous of fictional spies, James Bond. The drink is equal parts sweet and bitter, offering a unique flavor that you might not be accustomed to! If you're willing to try something new, you can see if the American ex-pats from whom it takes its name were onto something!

BASIC INGREDIENTS

 1 oz Campari

 1 oz sweet vermouth

 1 oz club soda

 1 lemon slice (garnish)

 GLASSWARE:
Old Fashioned glass.

1. Fill your glass with ice, then add the Campari and sweet vermouth. Top with soda water.

2. Garnish with a slice of lemon and enjoy!

CHERRY HOOKER

Like a more flavorful version of the Screwdriver, the Cherry Hooker is an orange- and cherry-flavored delight. With a little lime juice to add just a pinch of extra sourness, the Cherry Hooker is the sort of drink you might not ever think to make yourself, but once you taste it for the first time you'll wonder why not.

BASIC INGREDIENTS

 3 oz cherry brandy

 Orange juice to fill

 1 dash lime juice

 1 lime wheel (garnish)

GLASSWARE:
Mason Jar.

1. Add 3 oz of cherry brandy to a glass filled with ice, then fill the rest with orange juice.

2. Add a dash of lime juice. Stir thoroughly.

3. Garnish with a lime wheel and enjoy!

SNOWBALL

Never heard of Advocaat? Not surprising, since it tends to be more popular in the UK than the United States. Basically the European equivalent of eggnog, it's the perfect base for any winter warmer drink. The Snowball combines the citrus flavors of lemonade and lime juice with a little bit of maple syrup to create a sweet-and-sour winter treat.

BASIC INGREDIENTS

 I part Advocaat

 I dash lime juice

 I dash maple syrup

 I part lemonade

 I dollop whipped cream (garnish)

 I maraschino cherry (garnish)

 GLASSWARE: Mug.

1. Add the Advocaat and lime juice to a cocktail shaker filled with ice and shake thoroughly.

2. Strain the resulting mixture into your glass, then add maple syrup.

3. Top off the glass with lemonade and garnish with whipped cream and a cherry. Enjoy!

NON-ALCOHOLIC

You don't need alcohol to have a good time, and you *definitely* don't need alcohol to enjoy a delicious drink. In fact, as you might have noticed, a huge percentage of cocktails are based on trying to drown out the flavor of the alcohol rather than enhance it. With that in mind, why not just eliminate the alcohol and enjoy some delicious flavor combinations as they were meant to be enjoyed?

Over the course of the book, we've sprinkled in a number of alcohol-free alternatives to both new and classic cocktails. But don't worry—we won't make you flip through the whole book to find what you're looking for. We've got everything indexed right here!

Some of these mocktails are based on existing cocktails, while others are simply fantastic drinks that stand on their own. These drinks are perfect for a night when you just want to stay in, or when you want to go out without worrying about how you'll get home. Who needs booze? Forget cocktails—give these delicious mocktails a try!

CRIMSON LEMONADE

Lemonade and its dozens of variations provide a plethora of refreshing options for a hot summer day, but have you ever thought of adding a splash of grenadine? The subtle cherry or pomegranate flavor (depending on your preferred grenadine) adds a little hint of something more to this traditional drink, and the crimson color is a beautiful departure from the norm.

BASIC INGREDIENTS

8 oz lemonade

I splash grenadine

GLASSWARE:
Mason jar.

1. Pour lemonade into your Mason jar over ice.

2. Top with a splash of grenadine. Sit out on the front porch and enjoy!

SHIRLEY TEMPLE

Probably the most famous mocktail of all, the Shirley Temple takes a few classic secondary ingredients (grenadine and lime juice) and combines them with sweet ginger ale rather than alcohol. Perfect for both kids and adults looking to add a little extra flair to their soft drink, the Shirley Temple is as much an attention grabber as its curly-haired namesake was.

BASIC INGREDIENTS

 12 oz ginger ale

 1 splash grenadine

 1 dash lime juice

 1 maraschino cherry (garnish)

 GLASSWARE:
Highball glass.

1. Add ice to your glass, then pour in the ginger ale.

2. Top with a splash of grenadine and a dash of lime juice. Garnish with a maraschino cherry and enjoy!

ROY ROGERS

Arguably as famous as the Shirley Temple (although less adorably named), the Roy Rogers simply substitutes cola for the Shirley Temple's ginger ale. It's simple, tasty, and spices up an otherwise dull beverage. Who could say no to a little extra flavor in regular old cola?

BASIC INGREDIENTS

 12 oz cola

 1 dash grenadine syrup

 1 dash lime juice

 1 maraschino cherry (garnish)

 GLASSWARE:
Highball glass.

1. Add ice to your glass, then pour in the cola.

2. Top with a splash of grenadine and a dash of lime juice.

3. Garnish with a maraschino cherry and enjoy!

DRINK RECOMMENDATIONS

Need a little help expanding your tastes? Don't worry, we've got you covered. Just think of a classic drink you've enjoyed, and we'll let you know which recipes in this book that will scratch that same itch. Here are ten classic drinks paired with a few recommendations to get you started.

If you like the Old Fashioned, try: Manhattan, Rob Roy, Negroni.

If you like the Gimlet, try: Gin and Tonic, End of the Lime, Vodka and Tonic.

If you like the Mimosa, try: Screwdriver, Vodka Sunrise, Tequila Sunrise.

If you like the Cosmopolitan, try: Tropical Storm, Caribbean Cranberry Twist, Capescrew.

If you like the Margarita, try: Shot of Marg, Mexican Mule, Baja Lemonade.

If you like the Mai Tai, try: Your Tai, Vanilla Float, Island Punch.

If you like the Daiquiri, try: Daiquiri Twist, Gimlet, Margarita.

If you like the White Russian, try: Cuban Redhead, Snowball, Mocha Mocha Mocha.

If you like the Pina Colada, try: Cidermeister, Coconut Margarita, Banana Cream Pie.

If you like the Martini, try: Dirty Spy, Daiquiri, Gimlet.

TERMINOLOGY

BOURBON WHISKEY: A type of whiskey popular in the American South, distilled from a mash of at least 51% corn and aged in charred oak barrels.

COCKTAIL SHAKER: A sealed container used to mix cocktails by shaking. Usually filled with ice before use to quickly cool beverages.

DASH: A quick addition, usually of a liquid ingredient. Equal to approximately one teaspoon, but not an exact measurement.

DOLLOP: A large spoonful, usually in reference to whipped cream.

DUSTING: A small amount of a spice, usually in reference to cinnamon or nutmeg.

LIQUEUR: A sweet, flavored type of alcohol. Usually very strong in flavor and used as an accent in cocktails, rather than consumed on its own.

MIXING GLASS: A separate glass in which to mix ingredients together outside of the intended drinking vessel.

MUDDLE: Lightly mash ingredients in the bottom of a glass to better release their flavor. Can be done with any blunt instrument, but a specific tool known as a "muddler" also exists.

RYE WHISKEY: Similar to Bourbon Whiskey. Distilled from a mash of at least 51% rye and aged in charred oak barrels. Also refers to Canadian Whisky.

SCOTCH WHISKEY: A specific type of whiskey from Scotland, aged in oak casks for at least three years. The addition of peat smoke often gives it a smoky flavor.

SIMPLE SYRUP: Sugar water. For instructions on how to make your own, see the sidebar on page 69.

SLICE OF FRUIT: A common garnish. Refers to a slice taken from a fruit circle.

SPLASH: A quick addition, usually of a liquid ingredient. Larger than a dash, equal to approximately a tablespoon but not an exact measurement.

STRIP: A thin slice of rind taken from a citrus fruit.

TWIST: A strip of citrus rind sliced from around the diameter of the fruit to give it a twisted shape.

VIRGIN: Non-alcoholic.

WEDGE: A triangular slice of fruit (most commonly lime or lemon) used as a garnish. Often squeezed into the drink for added flavor.

WHEEL: A thin, circular slice of a fruit or vegetable. Most commonly used in reference to citrus fruits. Also known as "rounds."

RESOURCES

Looking for tools like cocktail shakers or mixing glasses? Look no further.

    http://www.cocktailkingdom.com/

    http://www.beveragefactory.com/

    http://www.barproducts.com/

For those in need of glassware, these fine retailers can provide you with everything you need.

    http://www.crateandbarrel.com/

    http://www.pier1.com/

Tired of ice melting and watering down your drink? Try some larger ice molds or whiskey stones!

    http://whiskystones.com/

    http://www.thewhiskeyball.com/

If you need flavored syrups for your drinks, you won't find anything better than the syrups at Torani.

    https://www.torani.com/

Want to learn more about cocktails? Try these fine resources for new ideas, how-tos, and educational material about all sorts of ingredients.

    http://liquor.com/

    http://cocktails.about.com/

For pitchers, punch bowls, and other party materials, check these great sites. Some even help you mix drinks right in the pitcher!

    http://www.bedbathandbeyond.com/

    http://www.webstaurantstore.com/

INDEX

ABOUT THE AUTHOR

Shane Carley, a longtime aficionado of all types of alcohol, jumped at the opportunity to launch a series of cocktail books. *The Home Bartender* is his follow-up to *The Mason Jar Cocktail Companion*. By day, he works as a copywriter for a New Hampshire university. Weekends, however, are spent on serious book research.

ABOUT
CIDER MILL PRESS
BOOK PUBLISHERS

Good ideas ripen with time. From seed to harvest, Cider Mill Press brings fine reading, information, and entertainment together between the covers of its creatively crafted books. Our Cider Mill bears fruit twice a year, publishing a new crop of titles each spring and fall.

Visit us on the Web at
www.cidermillpress.com

or write to us at
12 Spring Street
PO Box 454
Kennebunkport, Maine 04046